# Racial Influences on American Foreign Policy

# RACIAL INFLUENCES ON AMERICAN FOREIGN POLICY

*Edited by*

George W. Shepherd, Jr.

Basic Books, Inc., Publishers

New York, London

# Authors

RUPERT EMERSON received his Ph.D. in political science from the London School of Economics. He has taught at Harvard and Yale and has held administrative posts in the United States government. He has written *State and Sovereignty in Modern Germany, From Empire to Nation,* and *Africa and United States Policy.*

HAROLD R. ISAACS has had extensive experience as a reporter and is now a professor of political science at the Massachusetts Institute of Technology. His books include *The New World of Negro Americans, India's Ex-Untouchables,* and *American Jews in Israel.*

C. ERIC LINCOLN received his Ph.D. in social ethics from Boston University and is currently professor of sociology and religion at Union Theological Seminary. He has published *The Black Muslims in America, The Negro Pilgrimage in America,* and *Sounds of Struggle.*

JOHN MARCUM is a visiting professor of political science at the Graduate School of International Studies, University of Denver. He was awarded his Ph.D. from Stanford University. He has recently written *The Angolan Revolution Volume I: The Anatomy of an Explosion 1950–1962* and is now working on the second volume of the work.

JAMES MOSS received his Ph.D. in psychology from Peabody College. He was with the Bureau of External Research of the Department of State before accepting his present position as associate director of the Council on International Studies, State University of

New York at Buffalo. He is co-author of a forthcoming book on race in international relations.

ROBERT SCALAPINO, professor of political science at the University of California at Berkeley, received his Ph.D. from Harvard. He is co-author of *The Chinese Anarchist Movement* and *Parties and Politics in Contemporary Japan* and is the author of *The Japanese Communist Movement.*

PAUL SEABURY is a professor of political science at the University of California at Berkeley. He was awarded his Ph.D. in political science from Columbia. Among his publications are *The Wilhelmstrasse: A Study of German Diplomats under the Nazi Regime, Power, Freedom and Diplomacy,* and *The Rise and Decline of the Cold War.*

GEORGE W. SHEPHERD, JR., received his Ph.D. in political science at the University of London. He is currently a professor at the Graduate School of International Studies, University of Denver, and is director of the Center on International Race Relations. His publications include *They Wait in Darkness, The Politics of African Nationalism,* and *Nonaligned Black Africa: An International Subsystem.*

KALMAN H. SILVERT, professor of government and director of the Ibero-American Center at New York University, received his Ph.D. in political science from the University of Pennsylvania. He has written *Chile Yesterday and Today, the Conflict Society,* and *Guatemala: A Study in Government.*

# Acknowledgments

This collection is largely the result of a series of conferences that the Graduate School of International Studies has held on aspects of race in international relations, from 1967 to 1969. The author is grateful for the cooperation received from the contributors, who kindly revised their papers for this book. Funds for the initial conference were provided by the New World Foundation, and Josef Korbel, as Dean of the Graduate School of International Studies, contributed greatly in vision and support for the conferences and planning that led to this book. Other colleagues at GSIS, such as Charles Micaud and Joseph Szyliowicz, deserve special mention. And the able research assistance of Cyndi Kahn and Gail Schoettler has enabled this project to proceed rapidly. My associates in the Center on International Race Relations (CIRR), Tilden LeMelle and John Marcum, have also contributed both ideas and indispensable encouragement.

GEORGE W. SHEPHERD, JR.
Center on International Race Relations
University of Denver
*July 1970*

# Contents

# Racial Influences on American Foreign Policy

# Introduction

*George W. Shepherd, Jr.*

The white dominance structure based upon racial, cultural, and class distinction is disintegrating in our world today. With the fall of empires and the rise of liberation movements, all great powers must face the reality of racial attitudes in their policies. The United States, with its large nonwhite and non-Western minorities, is certainly no exception. To ignore this is to allow destructive subterranean forces to operate unrestrained. Alternative approaches to the problem, based upon a realistic assessment and recognition of the human values at stake, now need serious consideration.

This is a time of challenge to the old assumptions of a policy whose major article of faith has been serving the national interest, defined in terms of dominant Anglo-Saxon values and European ties. The myths of self-determination and democracy have frequently veiled the real goals of dominant group-interest and racial superiority. The staffing of our foreign service with the Anglo-Saxon products of the Ivy-League colleges, an immigration system favoring northern Europeans, and the economic exploitation of other races overseas testify to our dominant interests.

3

In recent years, however, such major social changes as the distintegration of empire and the collapse of the caste-color system have dramatized the necessity of reexamining the foreign policy of the United States. The emergence of various new nations following the breakup of empires led to a great deal of optimism concerning the prospects for national unity and development. Over the past two decades, American power has sought to facilitate this nationalism, but only as long as it did not directly challenge American interests. However, the outbreak of intense tribal and racial, as well as ideological, rivalries among groups has fomented civil war and created international confrontation. Under these conditions the United States has been caught in a complicated network of intrigue and forced to make choices between rival ethnic and racial groups. Unprepared and inexperienced in this kind of world, United States diplomacy has frequently been disastrous.

One major reason for these difficulties has been our continuous underestimation of the explosive potential of the racial factor. In Southeast Asia and Africa, for example, once the colonial administrations were withdrawn, the dynamics of rival group identity generated increased tensions. Malayans attacked Chinese; Hausa massacred Ibos; Africans revolted against Arabs; and white settlers enforced their control over black Africans. Racial prejudice was not the only obstacle to national unity but it greatly intensified hostilities based on economic and cultural differences. In recent years, therefore, preventing complete disintegration has become the major problem for many new nations. "Tribalism appears to be returning with a vengeance," [1] and many development plans have simply been shoved aside by the necessity of preventing a total governmental collapse.

Margery Perham a few years ago noted the central role of racial attitudes in the growth of African nationalism.[2] Arnold Toynbee has written of the danger of international racial warfare.[3] Until very recently, however, few American intellectuals other than the Black Power prophets such as W. E. B. DuBois have pointed to the significant influence of racist attitudes on relations among nations.

The collapse of white Western empires has coincided with the emergence from subjection of racial minorities in the United States, thereby simultaneously creating both an internal and an external racial crisis. Indeed, any hope for solution of either problem is inextricably linked to the other. It would be futile to direct all attention and resources from the international scene to the domestic or vice versa. Strategies against racism for the United States, caught in the midst of the crisis, must be seen simultaneously as global and local.

American black intellectuals in particular are challenging the traditional method of separating domestic from foreign problems. They see American racial problems as a form of colonialism.[4] This colonialism is perceived not only in discrimination and exploitation, but the entire American practice of assimilation is seen as analogous to the acculturation process of colonialism.[5] Thus many young American black leaders, because of their African heritage and their contempt for racism in America, have internationalized the racial issue. They have accepted the verdict of the seasoned Africanist Vernon McKay that "a principal impact of the rise of Africa has been its effect in transforming race relations into international relations." [6] Therefore the struggle for equal rights in the United States has become, for many political as well as academic blacks, a global liberation movement.

The development of such sentiments is of deep significance for an American policy which has always been sensitive to the influence of politicized minorities. However, its importance is still further extended by the simultaneous growth of nonblack political and intellectual movements which have also been concerned with enhancing opportunity and freedom in the United

States and abroad. This is most significant among the younger scholars who have been radicalized by the failure of Martin Luther King's dream at home, as well as by counterrevolutionary policies in Asia and Africa—policies which they see as the logical extension abroad of institutional racism.[7]

This collection of essays is one of the earliest products of the concern of established scholars who are beginning to examine more closely the role of racial institutions and attitudes in foreign relations.

Not all foreign policy analysts would agree with Gunnar Myrdal that there has been "a conspiracy of silence" about race in the study of South Asia.[8] Nor does the Black Power concept of institutional racism provide a completely adequate explanation. There are several other reasons for this belated American response to the world racial crisis.

Reluctance to confront the role of race in American foreign affairs is partly attributable to preconceptions long dominant in American thought. One such preconception focuses attention on the avowedly racist features of American society, primarily in the South, and assumes that non-Southern dominated institutions in America are free from discriminatory practices. Such a view has been challenged by the devastating evidence of the *Report of the National Advisory Commission on Civil Disorders,* which concluded, "Our nation is moving toward two societies—one black, one white—separate and unequal." [9] The Kerner Report pointed out that the problem of white racism cuts across the traditional concepts of North and South and pervades the entire American political scene. Given this reality, how can external relations be free of the effects of racial preference systems at home? The question must now be posed in a wider context than simply institutional racism, although this concept is a useful beginning.

Another preconception is based on the strong nationalist sentiment Americans have stressed from the beginning, that a plurality of origins has been assimilated into the American character. The suggestion that racial or ethnic differences are continuing stratification devices is threatening to the American dream. Just as the new nations of Asia and Africa have sought to suppress the multinational features of their new, unstable political systems, the United States process of political socialization, particularly after the Civil War and the great influx of immigrants in the late nineteenth century, has emphasized ideas that promote national unity. This political disposition was reinforced by a similar ethnocentric tendency among scholars. Functionalists in the study of nation-building abroad have emphasized order and unity just as American assimilationists have minimized conflict and ignored ethnic differences in favor of integration and unity.

American integrationists who have opposed a Black Power revival of Afro-American identity reflect the same acculturation discrimination found in the British and French civilizing mission. The conditional equalitarianism of Cecil Rhodes—"Equal opportunity for all civilized men and an equal opportunity for all to become civilized"—is based on similar assumptions concerning the superiority of white Western man's standards.

This ethnocentricism in Western development theories has been criticized for its "social Darwinism," [10] which assumes the absorption of so-called lesser and weaker cultures into the higher Western or Anglo-Saxon mold. Such cultural discrimination between racial groups is more accurately described as cultural racialism. Franz Fanon's attacks on the cultural racialism of the Western world have inspired a whole new generation of Third World liberation writers, from Vietnam and Algeria, who see violence as the only redeeming action for their lost manhood and unfulfilled national life.

The communist Chinese and Russians have been less successful in criticizing cultural racialism because of their own Messianic complexes, closely identified with national interests. Yet they have provided a great deal of support for the worldwide attack upon Western white dominance. In key points of revolutionary struggle, such as Vietnam and Algeria, their support to noncommunist liberation movements has had great impact.

The old verities that proclaimed the universality of Western political and economic models and implied the subordination of non-Western cultures and traditions have lost their automatic credibility. The way has thus been opened to more perceptive study of the special contribution of nonwhite and non-Western peoples within and among nations. The nineteenth-century Western racial arrogance of Hegel is being replaced by the pluralist modesty of Claude Lévi-Strauss, the French anthropologist.

Controversies over a definition of race and ethnicity have delayed the development of serious studies of race, especially in international relations, since it is here that the problem of distinguishing between culture or ethnicity and race is especially acute. Still, a general consensus has emerged among social scientists that makes it possible to investigate the racial phenomenon more effectively. Significant differences of interpretation still exist, as is apparent in these essays, and refinement is still a great problem, but these differences do not preclude a general agreement. Most race-relations specialists would now accept Peter Rose's definition that "a race is . . . a statistical aggregate of persons who share a composite of genetically transmissible physical traits." [11] There is also wide agreement on the utility of a social relations approach to race relations in the social sciences.[12] According to this view, race functions as a cleavage device, which, because of its genetic origins, differs from other societal cleavages based on cultural or economic group differences. But in all plural societies these cleavage devices are mutually reinforcing. Subordinate racial groups are kept in their inferior position by class and ethnic distinctions that reinforce the position of the dominant groups. Thus, for the social sciences, the study of race relations is primarily the examination of group relations in terms of the patterns of societal stratification brought about by perceived hereditary differences.

Race in foreign relations can be studied in numerous ways, but the purpose of the essays in this book is to describe the problem in general terms and to point up the ways in which race plays a role in American foreign relations, especially in the emerging areas. Our approach has been simply to survey the field and to raise issues. No attempt was made to present a common conceptual framework.[13] Specialists on American foreign relations and area studies were asked only to react to the existence and significance of the racial factor from the standpoint of their specialty. The imposition of a single conceptual framework, it was felt, would unnecessarily limit a wideranging examination of the problems and issues that provide an initial overview.

Most of these essays are based upon evidence that is not new; but the interpretation of this evidence contains many new insights into what are often ancient conflicts between racial groups. Moreover, the accumulated impact of these racial problems, when seen together, is overwhelming and dramatizes the immense significance they have for American foreign policy. This in particular has justified the compiling and editing of the present volume.

No pretense of definitive investigation is made here. Once the scope of the problem is seen as these essays depict it, in all its stark reality, then the serious student of foreign relations may be motivated to inquire further into ways of studying its ramifications.

Fortunately, there has been increasing ferment of scholarly activity relevant to the needs of foreign policy analysis, though little of it has been utilized to date. Race sociologists, such as Richard Schermerhorn and Pierre van den Berghe, have developed comparative methods for studying various types of national

racial systems. Guy Hunter has published a number of significant works, including his recent *Southeast Asia, Race, Culture,
and Nation.* These schemes and approaches provide a framework for future, more sophisticated political analysis. However,
this field has only begun to attract systematic studies.

In the study of foreign policy, the old dichotomy between
domestic and external politics is no longer valid, as James
Rosenau and others have demonstrated. Despite state protective
barriers, in the realm of communications and cultural developments, external influences increasingly penetrate across the
boundaries of the modern nation-state. One of these cross-
national linkages is the identity that racial and cultural groups
project. The importance of transnational loyalties for foreign
policy is great, as it touches the most sensitive security concepts
of the state.

Race is a transnational force in a variety of ways. Minority
ties to another fatherland or to an external racial group within
tightly knit ethnic and racial groups can create multiloyalties.
Thus, the study of race and foreign relations provides an especially useful means for understanding the interaction of domestic
and external political forces. Harold Isaacs' comprehensive article, "Race and Color in World Affairs," provides an excellent
survey of the immense scope of international race relations. He
links many of the conflict situations in Africa, Southwest Asia,
and Latin America to the internal domestic issues of race in
the United States, with particular attention to their influence
upon foreign relations.

In what is perhaps the most critical discussion of the collection, James Moss suggests that American foreign policy is dominated by a racist ideology. However, his views reflect a growing
school of black scholarship in this country, from Charles Hamilton to Eldridge Cleaver, whose challenges and propositions require further examination.

Paul Seabury presents what might be called the classic view

of the assimilationist pattern of American society. He outlines the significant points of influence that immigrant groups, especially the Irish, German, Jewish, and Eastern European minorities, have played. While he notes the controversy and instability caused by these interest groups, he asserts that they all have been Americanized and does not view the continuance of a cultural plurality as undermining the unity and basic objectives of American foreign policy. Nor does he see the role of the American Negro as moving outside this basic assimilationist pattern.

In contrast, James Moss maintains that the American Black, because of his racial differences, has not been allowed to follow the pattern of adaptation and acceptance of the Irish or German American, but has been locked out of the American dream and consequently out of participation at all important levels of American society, including foreign policy. Moreover, he sees the United States pursuing "a dual policy" in its foreign relations with the colored world. This, he believes, is contributing further to the alienation of the American Negro from American society and is intensifying his sense of identity with the people of color, especially his African brothers.

There are many topics that remain to be more fully examined in this controversy, many questions yet unanswered. Into what sort of foreign policy have the immigrant minorities been assimilated? According to the diplomatic historian James Bailey, the dominant American cultural perspective, from the Civil War through World War II, was Anglo-American. It can be argued that it still is. But diplomatic historians and other writers have given little attention to the inherent difficulties of assimilating non-white and non-Western groups into such a perspective. This, of course, immediately opens the issue of the vestige "Africanisms" that remain in the black diaspora within American society. If our society had allowed the American Negro to forget his color, he might also have forgotten his African heritage. But this has clearly not been the course of American social development. In addition to proclaiming that "black is beautiful," the militant American Negro is actively reviving the memories of his ancient past. Historians and cultural sociologists, not politicians, however, must settle these major questions through careful scholarship.

While there has been a great deal of empirical analysis of the voting behavior of American Negroes, no empirical work has been done on the role of the American Negro in foreign policy. This role should be examined at several levels, including the activities and influence of certain groups within the black community; the nature and extent of their representation in foreign policy; the involvement of Blacks in the decision-making processes; and the extent to which the black community benefits or suffers from external activities of this country, such as foreign aid and war. Unfortunately, this subject is not covered in the present collection.

It should also be noted that other nonwhite minorities, the Mexican, Arab, and Asian-Americans, have not been studied from this perspective. These minorities are considered only in terms of their domestic interests. The neglect of their external role is reflective of both the ethnocentric bias of scholarship as well as the subordinate status of these groups in American society.

The area articles in this collection serve primarily two useful functions. First, they demonstrate the growing significance of racial influences in the areas concerned which contribute to world instability. Second, in various ways they point to the inevitable involvement of United States policy in the racial conflicts and controversies of these areas.

With the withdrawal of *pax-Europa* from the colonial areas of the world, not only did new nations emerge, but new forces of racial conflict were also unleashed. In Asia and Africa, where minority racial and ethnic groups had long been suppressed by the centralized authority of colonialism and increasingly aroused by modernization, rivalries for power quickly formed along ethnic and racial lines. Robert Scalapino points out that in Southeast Asia, China, and Malaysia, ethnic differences became politically more potent in the postindependent period. The racial content of difference is perhaps most directly revealed in the long-standing rivalry between Chinese and Indians as immigrant groups in Southeast Asian societies.

Latin America has long been thought to demonstrate the prospects for racial harmony in the world. In an extremely provocative essay, Kalman Silvert exposes the subtleties of racism in the diverse countries of South and Central America. Racism, according to Silvert, correlates highly with, but is not equivalent to, economic stratification and the absence of national community. He examines the implications of these factors for American foreign policy by comparing the 1954 overthrow of the Guatemalan government with the Bay of Pigs fiasco in 1962.

Three of the nine articles in this collection deal with race in Africa. This disproportionate emphasis can be justified on the grounds that race relations between the nations of Africa and the United States may well become the most critical topic for American foreign policy. Not only are American Blacks increasingly finding a spiritual homeland in Africa—a sympathy which could develop into an effective lobby on behalf of African interests—but also the racial conflicts within Africa have the potential of involving the entire world.

Rupert Emerson, in his article, delineates the ethnic and racial rivalries that have proved so devastating in independent Africa, as most directly demonstrated in the Congo and Nigeria. The long-suppressed racial confrontation between Africans and whites in southern Africa has come to a head with the withdrawal of British power from central Africa and the unilateral seizure of power by the European minority in Rhodesia. My own contribution demonstrates that ethnocentric and racial conflict is as much a problem within and among African nations as it is between African and white nations.

United States involvement, by virtue of its diplomatic, military, and economic interests in these racial conflicts, is well brought out by John Marcum's analysis of southern Africa. The long-run implications of this for United States policy need to be given careful consideration. Does it mean, as Marcum suggests it does in southern Africa, an almost inevitable escalation of support for the dominant group in racial confrontations? Does this mean the United States will be drawn in on the side of the whites against the Africans in southern Africa (as we have already elsewhere), the Nigerians against the Biafrans, the Europeans against the Indians in Latin America, the Malayans against the Chinese in Southeast Asia? Marcum makes a convincing case for considering an alternative policy of disengagement in southern Africa. This is a thesis that needs careful exploration in both its practical consequences and its moral validity.

In all of these essays there are gaps. For example, very little attention is given to the problem of the Chinese in Indonesia, where, for a time, the dominant Indonesian government appeared to be pursuing a policy of genocide toward the Chinese population. The African essays make only passing reference to the problem of the immigrant Asian population in east, central, and southern Africa, though considerable treatment of this subject has been undertaken elsewhere. The severity of the Nigerian-Biafran war, resulting in the deaths of millions, raises the ominous prospect of massacre and genocidal civil war among the dense populations of Africa. Yet this problem is scarcely mentioned. None of the articles, with the exception of John

Marcum's discussion of United States policy in southern Africa, attempt extensive analysis of the policy problems for the United States raised by these racial conflicts. However, they do point up the situation and open the way for further inquiry and research.

The prospect of the United States becoming an arsenal for dominant groups in racial conflicts around the world is frightening. When cold war considerations penetrate racial conflicts, the possibility becomes still more real. The unhappy example of the British reluctantly supplying arms to the Nigerian government in its war against Biafran secession parallels United States policy dilemmas created by the conflict of interest with morality.

The feedback effects of such involvement on American society itself should also be considered. What happens in Africa, particularly in southern Africa, to Africans is of growing importance to American blacks. They are no longer disinterested bystanders to a Sharpeville Massacre or to the imposition of a white dictatorship on an African majority.

Pan-Negroism has been revived and basic questions have been raised about the racial biases of United States policy assumptions as well as white Western dominance systems. This response to the collapse of empire and the challenge to domestic racial discrimination is a stimulating and controversial beginning for new thought on race in American foreign policy.

The overwhelming impression that one gets from these articles is one of astonishment that the subject could have been neglected for so long. The facts have all been known for some time, but, like pieces of a kaleidoscope shaken in a particular way, it is only now that we see startling new patterns fall into place.

**NOTES**

1. Richard Schermerhorn in an unpublished paper. See his *Comparative Ethnic Relations: A Framework of Theory* (New York: Random House, 1969).

2. Margery Perham, *African Outline* (London: Oxford University Press, 1966), p. 51.

3. Arnold Toynbee, "Is a Race War Shaping Up?" *The New York Times Magazine,* September 29, 1963.

4. Stokely Carmichael and Charles Hamilton state: "Black people are legal citizens of the United States with, for the most part, the same legal rights as other citizens. Yet they stand as colonial subjects in relation to the white society. Thus institutional racism has another name: colonialism." *Black Power* (New York: Vintage, 1967), p. 5.

5. These assimilationist attitudes of even well-meaning liberal Africanists is deplored by black American Africanists. See articles by Tilden LeMelle "Where Was the Racism in Montreal?" and Herchelle Challenor "No Longer at Ease: Confrontation at the 12th Annual African Studies Association Meeting in Montreal" in *Africa Today,* 16, nos. 5 and 6 (October, November, December 1969): 3–4.

6. Quoted by Locksley Edmondson in his paper "Race and International Politics Since Versailles," *International Journal,* Autumn, 1969.

7. See L. L. Knowles and K. Prewitt, eds. (New York: Spectrum, 1969), pp. 11–13.

8. ". . . this conspiracy of silence on the race issue has, up till now, prevented all systematic empirical research about what goes on under the complacent public level." Gunnar Myrdal, "The Role and Reality of Race," address to Foreign Policy Association in New York City, April 1968, p. 7.

9. Tom Wicker, ed. *Report of the National Advisory Commission on Civil Disorders* (New York: Bantam Books, 1968), p. 1.

10. Ali Mazrui, "From Social Darwinism to Current Theories of Modernization: A Tradition of Analysis," *World Politics,* vol. 21, no. 1.

11. Peter Rose, *They and We* (New York: Random House, 1964), p. 8.

12. Michael Banton, *Race Relations* (New York: Basic Books, 1967).

13. We have begun this elsewhere. See "Conceptual Approaches to the Study of Race among Nations," in Symposium Papers (Denver: Center on International Race Relations, February 1969).

# 1 Race and Color in World Affairs

*Harold R. Isaacs*

## I

Matters of race and color are not actually more important in world affairs now than they were, say, a generation ago; only the thrust and direction of their importance have changed. This has been, of course, quite a change. The world of the 1940's was still by and large a Western white-dominated world. The long-established patterns of white power and nonwhite power-lessness were still the generally accepted order of things. All the accompanying assumptions and mythologies about race and color were still mostly taken for granted, hardly as yet shaken even by the Japanese challenge to Western primacy in Asia or by the attempt of the Germans to make themselves masters of the master race. The world of today is a world in which this white dominance no longer exists, certainly not in its old forms. The power system which supported it has crumbled. Its super-structure of beliefs about the superiority-inferiority patterns of races and cultures lies in pieces amid the ruins. While some people cling to chunks of the debris and stand defiantly in the door-openings of their shattered towers, most of us are stum-

19

bling blindly around trying to discern the new images, the new shapes and perspectives these changes have brought, to adjust to the painful rearrangement of identities and relationships which the new circumstances compel. This is now the pressing business of individuals, nations, and whole societies, and in the cluster of matters with which they must deal, hardly any is more nettling and more difficult to handle than the matter of race, especially as symbolized by differences of physical feature and color of skin. Of all the elements involved in this wrenching rearrangement, race or color is surely one of the most visible, more important in some cases than in others but in any case hardly not important at all.

Taking it in perhaps its largest aspect, we begin with the fact that the entire cluster of some seventy new states carved out of the old empires since 1945 is made up of nonwhite peoples newly out from under the political, economic, and psychological domination of white rulers. Our legacy from the fallen empires is a world now often seen as divided between the northern and southern hemispheres, between have-nations and have-not-nations, and in this picture all the haves, except the Japanese, are white, and the have-nots are all nonwhite, each bearing the heavy burden of the past with its experience of subjection or of mastery. To the political and economic tensions and conflicts that divide the world along these hemispheric and class lines, race differences and the recent history of racial behavior by whites add their own special quality of greater explosiveness. Indeed, among those who feel these differences most strongly—usually the angriest nonwhite radicals or the most frightened white conservatives—many are prone to put the race issue at the front and center of all current and prospective world conflict. Their prime threat or fear is the approach of a series of racial confrontations leading to a universal race war which will drive the line of color across all the other fields of conflict that now crisscross the globe. This is commonly foreseen as an apocalyptic collision between what Sukarno used to call the Oldefo (old established forces) under the leadership of the United States and the Soviet Union brought together by their common whitism, and Nefo (new emerging forces) led by China, mobilizing behind it all the peoples of the Third World united by their nonwhitism and their shared hatred of all whites. It would come as a crushing and catastrophic fulfillment of the famous prediction of W. E. B. DuBois of nearly seventy years ago, that the problem of the twentieth century would be "the problem of the color line—the relation of the darker to the lighter men in Asia and Africa, in America, and the islands of the sea," bringing a terrible time of reckoning for the white man called to account for his sins.

This may seem an unnecessarily feverish view of a world whose prospects just now are lurid enough under even the plainest light. But it will not do to dismiss it just because it is usually held in this form by racial extremists of one kind of another. This would be like dismissing as wholly implausible the notion that the United States would not have dropped on Germany the atom bomb it did drop on Japan, or speculation over the possible racial reasons explaining why a mercy airlift to rescue a handful of Europeans in the Congo was feasible while a mercy airlift to bring succor to thousands of dying Africans in Biafra was not. Even the most cogently argued explanations in both these matters could not entirely ignore their racial components. In any case, it takes only a slight jog of the kaleidoscope to produce a view of the future held by some quite sober citizens who believe that the necessary power arrangement to come— and possibly the ultimate nuclear showdown as well—must be a Russian-American combination against the Chinese, a prospect not as far removed from the race-war view as some of these sober citizens might want to insist it is.

But it is not necessary to be overcome by overheated visions of an oncoming race war to see that issues of race and color

are in some degree almost universally present in the great issues
and problems that dominate this hemispheric set of confrontations. These are mainly issues of resources and development,
population, and the shaping of the political institutions—more
open or more closed—that will govern the great majority of
men for a long while. Wherever the racial element is added to
national, class, religious, ethnic, and tribal lines of cleavage,
it brings its own peculiar accretion of greater glandular involvement and emotional violence to all the other elements of conflict in which we are now entangled.

## II

Race or color does not often appear as the central or single
most critical factor in conflicts affecting international relations.
As an issue of identity or relationship, it is more usually present
as one element among many. There are, however, some countries and situations where color does in fact figure as the core
issue making for both internal and external conflict. Of these the
most obvious and most important is the Union of South Africa.

The maintenance of white power by brute force in southern
Africa—taking in Rhodesia and South-West Africa—probably
supplies the main source in current reality for the vision of a
world eventually engulfed in a race war. If the actualities of
power in southern Africa and in black Africa have so far belied
the frequent predictions of explosive racial conflict there, this
hardly means that it will not come to pass at all. The chances
for that depend on whether the whites of Southern Africa do
finally come to their senses before it is too late, or whether
the black peoples of those countries will submit indefinitely to
their condition of total subjection. There is no present sign of
the first outcome and no basis for expecting the second. An
ultimately bloody confrontation of black and white in South

Africa, with all its possible, predictable, or imaginable consequences in the rest of the world and especially in the United
States, is by no means the least certain of all the grim possibilities that lie ahead for us all. It may be a nightmare of a
prospect, but as so much of our recent history has shown, night-
mares are a good deal more likely to come true than any of
our sweeter dreams.

But it is not only the possibility of future eruption that counts
in this measure of things. White power in Southern Africa is
right now probably the sharpest of all the wedges that separate
the newly emergent nonwhites from the whites of the world.
It continuously mobilizes the emotions, if not yet the effective
action, of the new nonwhite nations, especially in Africa, which
figure so prominently and yet so insecurely in the world's politics.
It may very well be that the South African mote blinds them
to their own racism or oppression of minorities, but the fact
remains nevertheless that the survival and blatant exercise of
white supremacy in South Africa keeps their own experience
with white racism alive and vivid. It provides them—and the
communist powers who are happy to be handed an additional
weapon—with a set of issues and emotions on which they can
all join despite so much else that divides them. Colonialism, often
used to serve the same purpose, may indeed be a dead horse—
except, to be sure, in Angola and Mozambique—but there is
nothing dead about white power as it is wielded in southern
Africa. It has appeared on the United Nations agenda every
year since 1952. Pushed by the nonwhite newcomers, often to
the acute discomfort of the British and the Americans, U.N. majorities have repeatedly denounced South African apartheid,
pressed the Southwest Africa issue, handed down detailed indictments of oppression of blacks and Indians, and demanded
international action to put down the South African and Rhodesian white racists.

The dragging reluctance of Britain and the United States to

join in these indictments—much less to take the actions voted—
has served as a measure in the minds of many nonwhites (American as well as others) of the value of the commitments which
these governments always make on the issues of equality and
justice in general. Those winds of change which blew away the
British Empire also have largely dissipated the sentimental-ro-
mantic fog that for a while overhung Britain's relations with its
ex-colonies. The influx of black and brown immigrants from
the Caribbean, India, and Pakistan has produced a full-fledged
white backlash in England, complete with riots, liberal dismay, civil-rights legislation, and restrictions on immigration. This
new state of affairs was dramatically underlined when the British
government recently reneged on its promise of an open door for
passport-holding Asian British subjects fleeing, ironically enough,
from black nationalism in Kenya. Britain's temporizing response
to white Rhodesian defiance has undoubtedly been due mainly
to Britain's post-imperial weakness, but African blacks and
Asian browns could quite reasonably interpret Britain's behavior
as not so much weak as white. In the case of the United States,
the equivocation over white racism in Africa helped to cancel
out the flickering sympathy the United States commanded at
times during the last ten years or so for its own turbulent and
only half-successful effort to do away with the survivals of white
racism at home. Into this equation must also go the size and
weight of Anglo-American investments and strategic-military
interests in South Africa, not to speak of the demonstrated over-
readiness of American power to intervene forcibly elsewhere
when its vital interests were thought to be involved. The overall
effect has been to reinforce in a general way the communist,
radical nationalist, and radical racialist views of Anglo-American
realities.

## III

Race or color is also a central or even governing factor in a number of other places and situations which may have less weight in the balance of world affairs but can hardly be seen as negligible in the working out of the next chapter of the human story.

Of these only Portugal's stubborn effort to keep power in its African colonies carries over what we might now call the old colonial pattern of things, although the Portuguese style of handling the color issue is several shades more ambiguous than that of its ex-counterparts elsewhere. Somewhat like the French colonialists, the Portuguese like to insist that they are a good deal more flexible in such matters, especially with nonwhites whom they coopt as willing instruments of white power, whether in bed, in politics, or in business. It is rather striking to note that the colonialists who have insisted most strongly on their paternalistic or racial flexibility as masters have tried the hardest or fought the longest and bloodiest wars to hold on to their colonies: the Dutch, the French, and lastly now the Portuguese. On the political side, no enduring vitality appeared in the methods and institutions by which they gave some limited voice to their colonials in their own affairs. On the racial side, there is little to support the claims of greater humanity that have often been made for themselves by the French, Dutch, and Portuguese colonialists as compared, for example, to the British. The differences are more a matter of style than of substance. Taking it in its most literal aspect, much waits to be learned about these differences from a comparison of the experience of the varieties of Eurasians and Eurafricans produced out of some of these colonial relationships. None of it seems likely to put any higher gloss on the picture we already have of this past. It is a matter of some suggestive relevance to our present theme, however, that the nationalist movement in Angola is reportedly split between at least two groups, one of which is said to be led by blacks, the other by mulattoes.

The other examples that fall into this category are in quite a different way part of our legacy from the colonial era. They all arise from the effort to create nations out of the often disparate and mutually hostile population groups which made up the former colonies where, as the saying went, division generally made for easier ruling. These differences are usually regional, tribal, and in highly varying degrees, "ethnic" or "racial," two vaguely defined terms used, for lack of more precise definition, to mark out some blurry lines between distinctions and differences that are sometimes physical, sometimes cultural, often both. Almost every "new" nation—and not a few "old" ones—is now more or less painfully hung on this kind of centrifuge.

Probably the bloodiest of these new confrontations where the difference is most distinctly racial is going on in the Sudan. Here a civil war has been under way since 1962 between the predominantly lighter-skinned Arab rulers in the north and the black non-Moslem people of the south, a clash in which this difference plays a paramount role. Another example was the heavy bloodletting between the tall Hamitic Watusi and the short Negroid Bahutu that accompanied the creation of the two small states of Burundi and Ruanda. Other situations with similar elements exist in several West African countries, like Sierra Leone, Gambia, and Liberia, where coastal "creoles" of varying degrees of racial mixture or foreign origin confront indigenous tribes in contests to hold or win power. There are north-south divisions in India which are demarcations of culture and language but also, to no small extent, divisions between light-skinned northerners and dark-skinned southerners with strong feelings about their lightness and darkness. Some of our "new" situations are filled with anomalies that in a number of cases have a strong racial cast, as in the encounter between European and Oriental

Jews in Israel, Arabs and Berbers in the Maghreb, Hindus and
Nagas in India's northeast, Hindus and Singhalese in Ceylon, the
"black" Khmers and the "yellow" Vietnamese. Also on this list
must appear the bizarre reproduction of older imperialist patterns by the neo-imperialist brown Indonesians in the imposition
of their rule on the black Papuans in West New Guinea.

If we were to extend this catalogue from the more distinctly
"racial" to the more vaguely "ethnic" or "tribal," it would obviously be possible to multiply examples almost indefinitely. In
cases where the colonial boundaries have been retained as national boundaries, again without regard for population groups,
conflict has been revived or ignited, both internally and across
borders, between peoples whose physical or racial differences
may be much less marked but between whom the ethnic or racial
clash is hardly any less intense. Consider on this score Nigeria,
the Congo, India in Assam and Nagaland, Indonesia in Borneo,
the Ethiopian-Somali-Kenyan irredentisms, the high perme-
ability of the frontiers of all the countries of the Indochina
peninsula, to say nothing of the presence of this factor on both
sides of the lines which arbitrarily divided North and South
Korea and North and South Vietnam, with rather notable effects
on American and world affairs.

Nor can we entirely fail to mention here—despite the absence
of the color factor as such—the long-vibrating hostility that
separates such European tribes as the Czechs and Slovaks, Serbs
and Croats, Flemands and Walloons, Welsh and Scots and
English, Bretons and French, French and English Canadians,
Spaniards and Basques, etc. The failure of so many political
systems—national, imperial, international—to satisfy the iden-
tity-needs of people in these many groups has led to the powerful
resurgence of feelings about their special separateness. Some
of these tribal differences have been bloodying the world's fields
for ages and we are plainly not done with them yet. However
else they are caused and defined, almost all are rooted in or

reinforced and rationalized by those physical and cultural differences which they themselves often see as "racial" or "ethnic" and which, despite all the mixing that has been done, manage somehow still to dominate so much of man's affairs.

There is, however, one group of "new" nations crippled by divisions of this kind which are in a peculiarly special way the most direct legacy from the colonial era. The largest and most internationally important of these is Malaysia, whose bi- or tri-racial character and consequent political and social fragility are mirrored in such smaller new states or microstates as Guyana, Trinidad and Tobago, Mauritius, Fiji (all former parts of the British Empire) and in Surinam, which is still a Dutch dependency. These are countries into which the colonial power deliberately imported working populations, either enlarging on older migrations or organizing new ones by large-scale contract labor, indenture or semi-indenture, in numbers large enough to become, in two or three generations, a significant minority, a plurality, or even a majority of the entire local population.

In one territory where this took place, Hawaii, a political solution was ultimately found in statehood within the developing framework of a new and uniquely American pluralism. In other areas, the option has had to be for nationhood, generally with much less hopeful results. In the Caribbean, this process began with the slaves brought from Africa ultimately displacing the indigenous Amerindians with a predominantly black population. When slavery was abolished, the freed blacks largely abandoned the land for the towns. The colonial rulers then brought in shiploads of more docile laborers for their plantations, in the main drawn from some of the lowest strata of the peasantry in India. The result today, in Guyana, for example, in a society composed of nearly equal parts of black Afro-Guyanese and brown East Indian Guyanese, whose differences, mutual antipathies, and conflicting interests have erupted in outbreaks of cruel violence as each group sought the uncertain prize of power in their rickety new national home.

Of considerably greater importance in world affairs, however, is Malaysia, a country of some eight million people at the tip of the Southeast Asian peninsula where the Indian Ocean meets the South China Sea at one of the world's major interoceanic crossroads. Here under the uncomfortably ill-fitting mantle of nationhood is a population made up of close to equal parts of Malays, who see themselves as the indigenous "sons of the soil," and Chinese, some of whose families have lived in the region for centuries but most of whom are products of the immigration begun in the last century when the British began to need workers more energetic than the pastorally inclined Malays. They also brought in workers from India for the rubber plantations, and Indians now comprise about 10 percent of the population. The bulk of the Malays remained poor farmers and fishermen while the Chinese came, in a generation or two, to control all sectors of the economy not dominated by the British. When the Japanese invaded in 1942, the Malays welcomed them and the Chinese resisted them, a difference that erupted in Chinese-Malay blood-letting just after the war ended. The communist-led uprising that kept the country in turmoil for about five years thereafter was a virtually all-Chinese movement. When in 1957 the assorted Malay states and sultanates were put together for the first time in their history as the new state of Malaya, the Malay princes, and other leaders negotiated Malay political dominance with the willing British. The Chinese, most of them uncertain or ambivalent about their hitherto firm political ties to their home-land, now a communist power, found themselves insecurely re-located as second-class citizens, accepted as nationals of the new state only under certain limitations and restrictions.

When Malaya was enlarged to become Malaysia in 1963, taking in the predominantly Chinese city of Singapore and the

North Borneo states of Sarawak and Sabah, the population also acquired sizable minorities of Dayaks and other tribes who shared an immense lack of any affinity—racial, cultural, or political—with either the Chinese or the Malays. The Borneo territory was brought in partly to offset the threat of an ethnic Chinese majority produced by the inclusion of Singapore. The mutual mistrust and hostility between Malays and Chinese forced the withdrawal of Singapore in 1965, which became an independent city-state on its own, leaving Malaysia still with a 40 percent Chinese minority. The cleavage between Chinese and Malays here is deeply cultural, having to do with history, language, religion, philosophy, and style of life. These are accented all the more by the racial and physical differences, including color, which mark them off from each other and which provide, as always, the handiest and most explicit basis for expressed hostility between individuals. On some satisfactory resolution of this conflict depends the viability of the Malaysian nation, and on this viability depends much that has to do with the bigger politics, the power alignments and positions, and the issues of war and peace among the larger powers whose interests meet or clash in that strategic corner of the world.


## IV


Far out beyond these small and localized blots of detail, changing color patterns are staining and rearranging the look of much larger areas of the new power-political map of the world. Besides the new and highly fluid patterns created by the north-south hemispheric view of the world to which we have already referred, there are also the triangular shapes created by that other hemispheric arrangement—East and West: the U.S.-Russian, Russian-Chinese, and Chinese-U.S. cleavages. In each of these combinations and often spreading through and across all of them run the feelings that have to do with race and all the attitudes, fears, self-perceptions, and mutual perceptions that go along with it.

The Soviet Union has long had to deal with race and color problems in its effort to create a successful federation of many diverse peoples, including the many nonwhites who make up the populations of the Soviet east. The dominance of the Great Russians in Soviet affairs has often had a racial as well as a national character. More recently the most visible outcropping of this kind in the Soviet Union has been the appearance of its own set of "yellow peril" fixations around its power conflict with China. The Russian-Chinese conflict has deep roots in the geography and history of these two huge continental powers. As in all such cases, mutual fears and hostilities are fed by racial differences which serve to reinforce or to rationalize politically dictated behavior. In recent years Russians have more and more openly expressed their feelings about Chinese in these terms. In conversations with Americans and Europeans, they frequently promote a common cause against the prospective Chinese threat in terms of a common "whiteness" united against Chinese "yellowness." They endow the latter with full-strength versions of all the most negative and fearsome stereotypes, bearing on numbers, limitless energy and endurance, fiendish cleverness and cruelty, deviousness, and inscrutability. These are all images they already hold in common with other Westerners, especially Americans, who get them from the same sources, indeed, from the same historic experiences. That Russians also share other varieties of "white" attitudes and behavior patterns toward nonwhites is amply indicated by the testimony of African students in Russia who met with discrimination, hostility, and violence at the hands of their Russian hosts and fellow students. Chinese students in Russia had similar experiences. However one might balance out the "facts" of these episodes, it is clear that some of this Russian "whiteness" is at least part of the story of the Russian failure to win allies and keep influential friends both in black Africa and yellow China.

In the case of China, its racial chauvinism has been a factor of great weight in communist Chinese political behavior, as it indeed has been in all of China's history. Chinese pride of place in the history and culture of the world is not easily separable from pride of race in its most literal physical form. Chinese feeling about the inferiority of all non-Chinese is almost always expressed in physical terms; outsiders are often portrayed as animals or animal-like demons, or are otherwise denied the status of human beings. It took a good deal of Chinese self-pride to sustain these convictions of Chinese superiority during the last century or so of repeated humiliation at the hands of foreigners. Repairing this damage to the Chinese ego and restoring the Chinese sense of greatness to its fullest luster are among the driving motivations of the present communist leadership in China. Although racism, at least crude racism, is anathema in communist ideology (as it is in the American credo), the Chinese, like the Russians, play heavily on its themes. They do so mainly negatively, charging their foes with its evils. Peking's heavy-handed and largely unsuccessful efforts to whip up support for itself in Africa and in the Third World movements associated with Bandung, Cairo, and Algiers were deeply—if informally—larded with racial arguments. In open propaganda, the Third World formula became a code for the "nonwhite world" counterposed to the white world of the United States and the Soviet Union. In their private maneuvering, it was specifically on racial grounds that the Chinese moved to keep Russia out of the councils of the Third World and to create an all-nonwhite international trade union movement which they could dominate.

The failures of this Chinese effort were, again, due to many causes: the actuality of Chinese weakness; the marked lack of enthusiasm among a great many Afro-Asians for Maoist extremism or for becoming tributaries to a new celestial empire; the counterweight of Western strength, resources, influence; or, often most powerfully of all, their own nationalism or their own values. But to judge from a variety of accounts, they also came about in part because the Chinese involved in these efforts could not help conveying their strong belief that, if Western whites were not superior to Africans and others, the Chinese were. We are far from through with Chinese chauvinism or with its racial component.

# V

For the United States most of all—more than for any other nation, new or old—the element of race and color has finally become a matter of central and crucial concern. Its importance cannot be separately assigned or portioned out between our internal or external affairs. In the fundamental sense that the role of the United States as a world power will be determined by the nature and quality of the American society, the United States itself has now become the principal arena of our struggle to shape the future. In that arena the principal issue, plainly put, is whether our partially opening society will open enough to include Americans who are black on the same common and equal basis as all others.

This is not to suggest that race and color did not figure importantly in our foreign affairs before this. Until twenty-five years or so ago, white supremacy was a generally assumed and accepted state of affairs in the United States as well as in Europe's empires. It did not begin to give way seriously in the United States until it had clearly begun to give way in the rest of the world. Until then, the notions of white supremacy and superiority and the subordinate position of blacks and other nonwhites in American society had been duly refracted in American affairs abroad. It showed up mainly in American relations with Asia where, in the middle of the nineteenth century, we joined Europe's freebooting imperialist system, acquiring our own "little brown brothers" in the process. Our behavior in these affairs was marked by that uniquely American combination of benevolence and rapacity, attraction and repulsion, virtue and cynicism which, for a great many Chinese at least, became our special national hallmark. At home in the United States during the same period we moved into an era of remarkable bigotry and violence against nonwhites. This was in the post-Reconstruction decades when nominally freed blacks were driven into new and even deeper pits of debasement. It was a period marked by the exclusion acts aimed at the Chinese beginning in 1882 and then against the Japanese. Not long thereafter came similar restrictions on all further immigration from anywhere except Anglo-Saxon northern Europe. The restrictions on Chinese and Japanese, including denial of the right to citizenship by naturalization, were continued until as recently as 1946. On the political side, we did not yield our extraterritorial position in China—won for us by European armed conquest a century earlier—until 1943. We are obviously not dealing here with matters of ancient or remote history.

The direct role of racism in these relationships and its effect on Asian-American relations during the last hundred years are almost always more or less consciously underplayed in American historical accounts. But there it is, barely out of view beneath the surface of most versions of our experience in the Philippines, where we were, to be sure, enormously benevolent, but where our soldiers sang about the monkeys who had no tails in Zamboanga. It is seen in the lynchings and other mob violence against Chinese in America; in the first antiforeign boycott in China in 1905, which was directed specifically against U.S. maltreatment of Chinese there; in the practice of discrimination against Japanese in the United States and its effect on Japanese-American relations before and after World War I, particularly in the negotiations at Versailles; and in the heavily race-tinted propaganda used by Japan against the United States before and during World War II.

Today this part of our past continues to dog us, mutedly in Japan just now, but quite explicitly in China, where communist propaganda against the United States makes heavy use of racial themes and images, not just because the Chinese are themselves racial chauvinists but because this kind of crude racism is no small part of what they had to take from us in the years of their weakness. It is still not easy for many Americans to understand that we are now simply getting quite a bit of our own thrown back at us, whether from China or Japan, from Latin America where the gringo syndrome carries its own special racial ingredient, or from Africa, in whose darkest experience of human enslavement we played such a prominent role.

But now the worms—and the wheels of history—have turned. The end of the system of white supremacy in the world, except in Southern Africa, has forced the quickening of the end of white supremacy in the United States. The changes that have taken place in this country in the last twenty years have come about for many reasons and as the outcome of many slowly— very slowly—converging forces and circumstances. But surely not the least of these was the sudden American need to deal as a great power with a world in which long-subordinate, submissive races had ceased to be subordinate or submissive. The racial facts of American life abruptly became vital to our success as leader, whether in pitting our claim of democratic freedom against the challenge of communist totalitarianism, or in winning the trust, not to say the alliance, of the new nations. It is hardly necessary to belabor this point at this late hour in the proceedings. It does not require too much distortion by our enemies to depict our destructiveness in Vietnam as a product of our disregard for nonwhite Asian lives. It does not require much imagination to guess how much more hopelessly untenable our position in Vietnam would be if we were claiming to fight there for Vietnamese democratic freedom of choice with an army that was still as racially segregated as it was when we fought for democracy and freedom in World War II, and as it remained until harsh military necessity imposed battlefield integration in Korea in 1950.

Through the 1950s and early 1960s, these issues were dramatized by repeated incidents in the United States involving newly arrived black and brown diplomats from the recently independent nations, who were constantly being caught in the still-prevailing patterns of discrimination and exclusion in hotels, restaurants, and other public places as well as in housing in New York, Washington, and elsewhere. The embarrassed apologies to the diplomats involved and the exhortations addressed to recalcitrant white Americans about these episodes must fill a large file at the State Department and at the headquarters of the U.S. delegation to the United Nations. It is not far wrong to say that the desegregation of many of these places was largely won in the first instance because nobody could ever be sure any more that a reasonably well-dressed dark-skinned man who came seeking service was not the Ambassador from Ghana or India, an outcome that served only to deepen the humiliation and anger of dark-skinned men or women who happened to be just ordinary Americans who wanted that service too.

Much more dramatic was the turmoil set in motion by the Supreme Court decisions and the early racial clashes in the schools and universities, at the lunch counters, in terminals and other public places. The events of this period commanded the fascinated attention of a world that had never seen anything like it: the Negro rebellion launched by Martin Luther King's walkers in Montgomery in 1955; federal soldiers and marshals enforcing compliance with the law on southern white racists at

Little Rock, Tuscaloosa, and elsewhere; the sit-in movement and the freedom rides; the civil-rights laws finally pushed through a reluctant Congress; the climactic confrontation at Birmingham; and the tardy but unmistakable commitment of the Kennedy Administration in 1963 to see the issue through. All of this on balance offset the uglier scenes that even then were cast so widely on all the world's screens. There remained the image of a society finally moving to cope with some of its most deep-seated problems, and doing so more boldly and more openly than any other nation in a world where scarcely anyone was free to cast stones.

In the last five years, the picture has cruelly changed. Belief abroad in the relative virtue or morality and—perhaps even more decisive—even in the intelligence of American behavior as a world power has been largely shot away in Vietnam. At home, the civil-rights revolution, having cleared the barricades of legal segregation, came up against the much more difficult problem of achieving a decent existence freed of the shackles imposed by poverty, of overcoming the rot of our inner cities and the persistence of strong racial attitudes and behavior in large sections of the surrounding white population. Negro hopes of change raised by the swift victories of the civil-rights revolution have given way to deep frustration that often seeks an outlet in bristling ultramilitancy and a profound skepticism about the society's good intentions. Hopes of many Negroes in the promises of integration have given way to despairing impulses toward some new kind of separation. For large numbers of white Americans, especially among the young, much of the same faith has been buried in the Vietnam morass, while in other large sections of the population a nascent readiness to accept change in race relations has been obscured by the angry and fearful resurrection of old racial spectres spurred by outbreaks of violence in the ghettos. The crisis now wide open in American life is a concatenation of long-unsolved problems of poverty, the cities, and race, each formidable enough in itself but woven together now in a single massive tangle of issues, demands, and circumstances.

Of the three, the most critical is clearly race. To see that this is so, one has only to imagine what our present national condition and state of mind would be if our poor, especially in our city slums, were not so largely black. Without the problem of race, we would be facing demands of the kind this society has shown itself matchlessly able to confront and solve. It is the demand that we finally resolve the place of the black men in the American society that makes this the potentially mortal climax of an issue that has been with us since the founding of the Republic. It bears on what our society is and on what we say we think it is or want it to be—namely an open society offering freedom of choice and growth and well-being to all its citizens regardless of race, creed, color, or national origin.

There has been no such society on earth and the American promise of it is in fact the unique substance of the American alternative to the claims of the communist totalitarians. It is the difference between the promise of our open society and the closed society of the communists that makes the world power struggle something more than a matter of deciding an issue of brute force. It can, of course, be argued that American power will impinge heavily on the world no matter what is done about the place of the black man in American society. This is no doubt so. But the proposition here is that the world power role and impact of an American society on its way to becoming an open, humane society for all its members is one thing. The role and impact of an American society moving toward new forms of racial separation in a garrison state will be quite another.

# The Race Problem and International Relations

2

*C. Eric Lincoln*

In the spring of 1964, at the request of the State Department, I did a tour of certain European capitals lecturing at various universities and before other groups interested in American race problems. The official title of my lecture series was "Social Change in a Democratic Society." The unofficial title was "What the Hell's Going on in Selma, Alabama, and Why!" The lectures were necessary, or at least expedient, as a function of the State Department's constant effort to shore up a chronically deteriorating political position deriving from the worldwide knowledge of worsening race relations here in the United States at a time when we were crucially involved in a struggle for leadership in the free world. Traveling with me was Attorney Wiley Branton, formerly chief counsel for the Little Rock Nine who integrated Central High School under the protection of federal troops in 1957, and who was to become later the very resourceful director of the Voter Education Project in the South.[1] A sociologist and a lawyer, we were billed together as a team, both practically and theoretically involved in the dramatic and painful social change which was shaking the very foundations of Western democracy.

We were late. Much damage had already been done. A thousand pictures in a thousand newspapers across the cities and towns of Europe, Asia, and Africa had given an irrevocable concept of the social depravity of America. The faces of hatred that obtruded themselves into the range of the cameras at Little Rock and Oxford were, when they were shown to us in Europe, undeniable representations of an ignoble and undemocratic aspect of American character. The camera and newspaper scenes were visual. They were substantial and real. In comparison to the hate-distorted faces of the women who screamed and spat and cursed and threw rocks at Little Rock and New Orleans, the snarls on the faces of the dogs at Birmingham and Selma seemed more human, more humane. Neither Mr. Branton nor I could by any stretch of imagination be considered apologists for the federal government or for the American people. Nevertheless, too often our analysis was lost altogether or seriously devalued in the preconceptions derived from the daily news, which offered vivid contradictions to our more disciplined and objective presentations.

In spite of the almost universal recoil of Western Europe from the murder and lawlessness which have illustrated our attempts at social change in the South for the past decade (and most particularly the sustained savagery which occurred at Birmingham and Selma), it was apparent that Europeans generally felt a genuine compassion for (and perhaps a vicarious involvement in) the social travail which racked the American people. Again and again they cheered Martin Luther King and the heroic, disciplined efforts of the American Negroes to free themselves and become men among men, but they were more saddened than reproachful that the opposition to Negroes' realization of full freedom in America was made up of the very (white) Americans to whom they looked for world leadership, and implicitly, the preservation of their own freedom. There was an almost sentimental willingness to believe that the American government would "do the right thing," and that the American people, conscious of their international political responsibilities, would soon come to accept the inevitability of change.

The French-speaking West Africans we met in Paris and in London were considerably less certain of any manifest destiny for America in world politics, and even less confident in the sincerity of the federal government's efforts on behalf of its Negro citizens. At the American Institute in Paris an African scholar from a former French colony denounced the nonviolent movement of Dr. King as "stupid and degrading" and denied that there was "any precedent anywhere in the history of Western civilization to suggest that the white European could be or has ever been moved to moral behavior by the voluntary prostration of the black man." His "solution" to the race problem in the United States was the "bombing of courthouses and post offices, warehouses and bridges until the Negro dissidents are recognized as a revolutionary force to be reckoned with." Since that time we have had Watts, Chicago, Rochester, Omaha, and a dozen other bombings and burnings initiated by "Negro dissidents." We have also something called "Black Power" which is as suspicious of the white man's intent in general, and the federal government's intent in particular, as was the French West African.

We *are* concerned about what other people think of us or we would not spend the millions we do spend to maintain information agencies, libraries, and radio stations around the world. We are more concerned now than ever before about a better image in race relations. Our present emphases reflect the new social and political realities of the world in which we live, but the race problem in international relations is at least as old as the American republic itself. Indeed, it antedates the American Revolution, and it is one of the ironies of history that the problem was first laid at the door of British arrogance as being foisted upon an unwilling and unsympathetic colonial population in the form of African slavery. By the opening of the last quarter of the eighteenth century as British-American interests became increasingly strained, the continued traffic in slaves became so obnoxious to some of the colonists that an agreement in the Continental Congress in the fall of 1774 prohibited the importation of slaves after December 1, 1775.[2]

Reflecting what he doubtless thought to be the prevailing sentiment, Thomas Jefferson wrote "A Summary View of the Rights of British America" in which he claimed that the abolition of slavery was greatly desired in the colonies, but that the humane objectives of the colonists were continuously blocked by British policy. But Jefferson overestimated the anti-slavery enthusiasm of his compatriots, for when in his initial draft of the Declaration of Independence he charged the British king with having:

> . . . waged cruel war against nature itself, violating its most sacred rights of life and liberty in the persons of a distant people who never offended him, captivating and carrying them into slavery into another hemisphere . . . (and having) prostituted his negative for suppressing every legislative attempt to prohibit or restrain this execrable commerce . . . paying off crimes committed against the liberties of one people, with crimes which he urges them to commit against the lives of another. . . .[3]

the visionary Jefferson found himself at odds with the materialistic interests of the southern delegation who persisted in having all mention of the slave trade stricken from the declaration.

This was perhaps the first time the race problem had entered into American international relations.

Another early portent of the unremitting trouble and embarrassment the race problem was to cause the United States was the use of Negro soldiers in the war for independence. George Washington himself once predicted that the Negroes in America would become "a troublesome species of property" as the generations succeeded each other. History has confirmed his clairvoyance, for as "property" and as "people," they have indeed been a troublesome irritant of the domestic tranquility, and an annoying diffraction of our image abroad.

Washington's questions on the use of Negro soldiers were prompted by the consciences of some colonials who felt it somehow inappropriate to the spirit of justice to allow Negroes to die for a freedom in which they were to have but scant, illusive participation, if any at all, and by the more practical issue of whether the British would use Negroes as soldiers if the colonies did.[4] Washington and his advisors—including Major Generals Ward, Lee, and Putnam, and Brigadier Generals Thomas, Spencer, Heath, Sullivan, Greene, and Gates—were unanimous in their desire to keep it a white man's war on both sides.[5] It is one of the ironies of American history that well before General Washington assumed command of the colonial forces, Negroes had already distinguished themselves at Lexington, Concord, and Bunker Hill; and indeed, Crispus Attucks, a runaway slave, had been the first American to give his life for American independence at the Battle of King Street five years earlier. "From that moment," Daniel Webster was to say, "we may date the severence of the British Empire."

In spite of all this, and in spite of the fact that a good number of free Negroes (and probably some slaves) were already under arms, Washington's council of war, supported by a civilian committee which included Benjamin Franklin, Thomas Lynch, and the deputy governors of Rhode Island and Connecticut, issued an order on November 12, 1775 barring the enlistment of Negroes, slave or free. A quick reversal of policy was forthcoming when it became known that Lord Dunmore, the British governor of Virginia, had five days earlier issued a proclamation inviting all Negroes, slave or free, to join his Majesty's troops "for the more speedily reducing [of the rebel colonies] to proper dignity." Washington, of course, recanted, and Congress subsequently approved the enlistment of free Negroes. Most of the individual states went even further—many of them enacting specific legislation to permit the enlistment of slaves as well as free men of color.[6]

Such was the inauspicious beginning of a foreign policy which has ever since required a peculiar recognition of America's peculiar problem. As the passing years have become history, the problem has not abated. Indeed it has grown more monstrous in character, more difficult to control, and impossible to conceal. On the other hand, it is also more difficult to document than in the early days of the republic. Our contemporary statesmen are more sophisticated and perhaps less troubled by matters of conscience than by a certain expediency that returns them to office. The political stakes are often bigger than the welfare of colored minorities. Then, too, we are closely allied with a whole confraternity of nations whose recent past is stained with the scarcely dried blood of colonialism. We have high economic and political stakes in some countries for which racial oppression and exploitation without apology is a determined, world-defying way of life. In this regard, we and the world are aware that without our support, direct or indirect, and without our approval, tacit or articulated in whatever kind of diplomatic jargon, no nation now following an overt policy of racial oppression could long sustain itself or its policies. International diplomacy has become largely a matter of personal commitments between heads of state or their personal representatives. But now we must also reckon with the fact that civil-rights groups can bring to bear an ever-increasing amount of political power at home, making it politically hazardous for any American foreign policy with racial overtones to become public knowledge. All these factors make it extremely difficult to document satisfactorily the impact of the race problem on contemporary international relations. There is, of course, a great deal of speculation—informed and uninformed. But hard data are difficult to come by.

An incident which developed during World War I, for example, could hardly take place today. At the beginning of that war there was a great deal of opposition from southern politicians to the drafting of Negroes into fighting units of the regular army, and particularly to their being sent overseas, where it was feared that they might have experiences which would make them dissatisfied with the status they occupied at home. The American armed forces of World War I were segregated; and the American military establishment longed so desperately to universalize those prejudices that it attempted to impose them by directive upon the military personnel of at least one sovereign foreign power (France). In a document entitled *Secret Information Concerning Black American Troops* issued by United States Army authorities in Paris, the following were included among instructions offered the French Military Missions regarding their proper relations to Negro troops:

> "there would be no intimacy between French officers and Black officers," it stated. "We must be courteous and amiable with these last [i.e., blacks] but we cannot deal with them on the same plane as with white American officers without deeply wounding the latter." Further, "We must not eat with them, must not shake hands with them or seek to meet with them outside the requirements of military service."
>
> The directive also stated, "We must not commend too highly the black American troops, particularly in the presence of white Americans. . . . Make a point of keeping the native cantonment population from 'spoiling' the Negroes . . . White Americans become greatly incensed at any public expression of intimacy between white women and black men." [7]

While it may be argued that this racial backbiting was not the "official policy of the United States government," it was certainly the official policy of the United States military, and as such it was intended to influence in a significant way the international relations of the country as a whole. The matter was exposed by W. E. B. DuBois, then editor of the *Crisis Magazine,* the official organ of the NAACP.[8]

Perhaps the most dramatic instance of official American concern with the effect of domestic race relations on international policy prior to World War II developed with our deep apprehension about the Garvey movement of the 1920s. It is, admittedly, a concern most difficult to document now, forty years or so later. Nevertheless, the fact remains that Garveyism generated a black following (which Garvey numbered at more than three million, and which in any case could hardly have been less than 500,000), more than enough to become a matter of international uneasiness. Garvey's headquarters were in New York City, where at the First International Convention of his Universal Negro Improvement Association in August 1920, the black populations of twenty-five countries were represented, and Garvey's opening address was heard by 25,000 people.[9] Since the UNIA was essentially black zionism, designed to lead the Negroes of the Western world "back to Africa," it found great favor with the local white racial conservatives of the day. The problem in international relations arose when it began to appear that the ludicrous little Jamaican who called himself the Provisional President of Africa might actually attempt to establish a colony on that continent.

President Edwin Barclay of Liberia, with whom Garvey was negotiating for a beachhead, promised to "afford the Association every facility legally possible in effectuating in Liberia its industrial, agricultural and business projects." But Barclay also felt moved to inform Garvey that "The British and French have inquired. . . . It is not always advisable nor politic to openly expose our secret intentions," the Liberian president went on. "We don't tell them what we think; we only tell them what we like them to hear—what, in fact, they like to hear."[10]

Garvey himself felt no need for caution. He declared in a

public address: "We say to the white man who now dominates Africa that it is to his interest to clear out of Africa now, because we are coming . . . 400,000 strong. . . . We shall not ask England or France or Italy or Belgium, 'Why are you here?' We shall only command them, 'Get out of here.' " [11]

By 1924 the Garvey movement was growing from strength to strength. It had a full slate of officers in its provisional cabinet, a provisional president, a flag, a provisional army, a steamship line to transport people of African descent back to Africa, a flying corps, a motor corps, a nursing corps, a religious order built around a black God and a black Madonna-and-Child, and a newspaper printed in English, French, and Spanish with a circulation throughout the Negro world in Africa and the United States, as well as Central and Latin America. And it had the promise of land in Liberia. The European colonial powers became alarmed and communicated their concern to the American government as well as to its Liberian protectorate. Suddenly in the summer of 1924 the Liberian government (which had welcomed several Garvey missions—one as late as June 1924—and whose mayor of Monrovia had accepted the post of Secretary of State in Garvey's provisional government) sent a diplomatic note to the United States announcing that it was "irrevocably opposed both in principle and in fact to the incendiary policy of the Universal Negro Improvement Association headed by Marcus Garvey." Furthermore, the lands promised Garvey were now leased instead to the Firestone Rubber Corporation.[12] Soon after, Garvey was imprisoned on an old charge of using the mails to defraud in the promotion of his steamship line. He was convicted in February 1925 and sent to federal prison in Atlanta, where he remained until his sentence was commuted by President Coolidge in 1927.

Garvey's enemies were many. Among his bitterest opponents were the "respectable" Negro leaders of the day who made trouble for him whenever they could. But the Universal Negro

Improvement Association was a mass movement of international proportions, and as such, at the time of its zenith, too big to be seriously affected by the limited power of the established Negro leadership. We can only surmise from the scant evidence available that the influence of the Garvey movement came to an abrupt end throughout the black man's world because it was escalated to a high place on the agenda of international relations, and American diplomacy did not shrink from its indicated task.

The race problem in America did not really gain significant status in the definition of American foreign policy until the end of World War II. America's problem is essentially a problem of black people subjugated by white people, a not unfamiliar phenomenon in the last three hundred years of Western history. The nations with which we maintained diplomatic relations were white nations, which like ourselves were engaged in exploiting nonwhite peoples. There was little reason to be concerned about our image abroad with reference to racial abuses at home. We were all members of the same international club. What is more, our image-makers felt no need to be concerned about our racial behavior abroad insofar as that behavior might be obnoxious to the nonwhite minority at home. From the mid-nineteenth century on, there were, with the possible exception of Japan, few sovereign, nonwhite peoples of any consequence left anywhere in the world. Ever since the French Revolution the doctrine of superior and inferior races had continued to gain strategic adherents all over the world, and for many a Western nation, racism as a policy was implicitly if not explicitly adopted as a decision-making reference in foreign and domestic affairs.

Nevertheless, here in the United States, since the beginning of the convention movement in the early 1830s, Negroes have been engaged in a forlorn and bitter struggle directed toward the elimination of color as the chief criterion of individual worth. Even in the face of that unimaginative judicial decision in the case of *Plessy* v. *Ferguson*, which in 1896 plunged the country into a half century of legal discrimination, not only did the Negro American continue the struggle for his own liberation, but he also shortly took up the cause of freedom for his African brothers whose thralldom was in many ways worse than his own.

From around 1900 onward, when they themselves were little more than a generation out of absolute slavery, and far from being truly "free," Negroes in America displayed a progressive interest in Africa and did what they could to improve the lot of the African and to make his yoke lighter. That this is so is all the more remarkable in that seldom in his long history in America did the American Negro have available to him either a favorable or even a reasonably accurate stereotype of African culture or personality. Despite this severe gulf that separated him from his African counterpart, the American Negro, to the extent of his limited resources, shouldered the African's burden—at least psychologically and symbolically—with his own. With some charity we can declare that the American writers who go to such lengths to make it appear that Africans and Negro Americans have always had mutually exclusive interests have either not given proper examination to the data available, or they have misread it.[13]

At a Pan-American Congress which met in London in July 1900, William Edward Burghardt DuBois, chairman of the Conference's Committee on Address to the Nations of the World, articulated for the American Negro his feelings and his concern about Africa and Africans when he challenged the colonialism that was a near-universal feature of European civilization by demanding:

Let the British Nation, the first modern champion of Negro freedom, hasten to . . . give, as soon as practicable, the rights of responsible government to the Black Colonies of Africa and the West Indies.[14]

The first of five Pan-African Congresses which together constitute the modern movement, and which played an important role in African independence, was convened in Paris in 1919 a few miles from where the Peace Conference was sitting in Versailles. It is revealing that President Woodrow Wilson tried to prevail upon French Premier Georges Clemenceau to send DuBois home. Acting Secretary of State Polk had already assured the American people that the French government advised the State Department that no such conference could be held. The State Department accordingly refused to issue passports to Negro delegates from the United States who wished to attend.[15] However, Clemenceau called in Blaise Diagne, the black French deputy from Senegal, and after being assured by Diagne that the conference was not designed to sow disaffections among French African troops, Clemenceau permitted it to proceed despite State Department objections.[16]

Among other accomplishments, the conference drafted a petition urging the allies to place the former German colonies in Africa under international supervision against the day when they would become self-governing. A diluted version of this proposal was subsequently incorporated into the mandate system of the League of Nations.

Other Pan-African Conferences met in London, Brussels, and Paris (capitals of the leading European colonial powers) in 1921; London and Lisbon in 1923; New York City in 1927; and Manchester, England in 1945. At the 1945 meeting, names like Kwame Nkrumah, Jomo Kenyatta, and Nnamdi Azikiwe were prominent in the affairs of the Congress. Formerly largely the voice of the American Negro (led by W. E. B. DuBois), Pan-Africanism had now come of age and would soon express itself in the nationalism that was to gain most of Africa her freedom.

In 1935, when Italy embarked on its infamous "rape of

Ethiopia," Negroes in the United States boycotted Italian merchants, and Negro leaders made representations to the federal government. Citizens' organizations were set up to aid Ethiopia, and a delegation of American Negroes attended the International Peace Campaign in Brussels in 1936.[17] Although their accomplishments were not impressive, the Negroes in America did seek to dramatize their sense of meaningful concern over the fortunes of black men elsewhere in the world who shared with them a related, if not an altogether common, fate. That concern has increased rather than diminished. As recently as 1962, some of the country's most distinguished Negro leaders met at Columbia University as "The American Negro Leadership Conference on Africa," and in Washington, D.C., in 1965 to express solidarity with the African community, and to call upon the federal government to reexamine its policies toward the African states in the light of what appeared to be a preeminent concern for Western Europe. A preamble to a list of resolutions made at the first Leadership Conference declares:

> The American Negro community in the United States has a special responsibility to urge a dynamic African policy upon our government. Although we have a serious civil rights problem which exhausts much of our energy, we cannot separate this struggle at home from that abroad. If the United States cannot help win freedom in Africa, we cannot expect to maintain the trust and friendship of the newly-independent and soon-to-be independent peoples of Africa and Asia.[18]

Among the resolutions offered was one which deplored "the use of any arm of our government to protect those who are working against the interests of the people of the Congo, Angola, and Mozambique." Another deplored "our government's opposition to the United Nations resolution calling for sanctions against South Africa," while a third urged "the American government to insure that no arms, weapons or war material supplied to Portugal by the United States are used against the people of Portuguese territories in Africa in its efforts to keep the people in subjugation." [19]

Whether the federal establishment was impressed to the point of modifying any of its policies toward Africa can only be guessed, but it *was* impressed enough to send no fewer than sixteen observers from the State Department to the Second Conference meeting in 1964, as well as other observers from the Agency of International Development and the United States Information Agency. No doubt encouraged by this indication of concern, the conference recommended the establishment of a permanent body to carry out its aims and purposes, prominent among which was the establishment of a lobby in Washington.

The Pan-African Movement could well have been interpreted by careful political observers to mean that responsible Negroes in the United States were gradually accumulating a community of experiences with their African counterparts that could only lead to increased mutual respect and concern. The Negro's unremitting battle for integration at home has been grossly misinterpreted as the absence of concern for nonwhites elsewhere in the world, especially in Africa. Such thinking is indicative of the superficial nature of the contact between Negroes and their interpreters, and it reflects the stereotyped thinking about what Negroes want, or ought to want. The American Negro does, of course, give priority to the improvement of his own status at home. So do all other civilized people, and such a priority is obviously necessary if he is to win a position from which he may realistically expect to be of definitive help to others who are also struggling against the constraints of various forms of racism.

The riot in the gallery of the United Nations in February 1961 represented an emotional overflow experienced by Negroes who saw in Patrice Lumumba the African counterpart of countless numbers of Negroes who have been martyred in America. Said one observer:

> The demonstrators in the United Nations gallery interpreted the murder of Lumumba as the international lynching of a black man on the altar of colonialism and white supremacy. Suddenly, to them at least, Lumumba became Emmett Till and all the other black victims of lynch law and the mob. The plight of the Africans still fighting to throw off the yoke of colonialism and the plight of the Afro-Americans, still waiting for a rich, strong and boastful nation to redeem the promise of freedom and citizenship, became one and the same.[20]

The U.N. disturbance caught American diplomacy off guard. In the matter of African colonialism, our national policy has been to run with the hare and hunt with the hounds, and if our two faces have been obvious, we have been more concerned about maintaining our "friendships" with nations owning militarily strategic plots of real estate than we have with minority-group opinion at home. In short, in times past, the sensibilities of our homegrown Negroes have scarcely been a major factor in structuring our international policy. There is some indication that change is in the air.

There is what novelist John O. Killens calls a "Brotherhood of Blackness." This "brotherhood" has no necessary relationship to black nationalism, or Pan-Africanism, or to any kind of political unity based on race. It is, says Killens, "the Fellowship of the Wretched and Disinherited." Membership is involuntary and is a necessary derivative of being black in a world ruled by a white hegemony.

> We have been for centuries the victims of White Supremacy, that fountainhead of the Western Judeo-Christian world. White Supremacy brought the club together all over this unhappy earth, and designated the members of the Brotherhood as "niggers." It

was the Great Recruiter. But now the time is long past for us
to call the meeting of the Brotherhood to order, the first order of
business being the bringing about of the downfall of our
Founder.[21]

What Killens is saying in this monologue on blackness is that
Negroes in America know, or at least some of them know, that
their problem is more than a matter of local acceptance by the
neighborhood PTA. It is a problem of an attitude that is not
reserved for them because they are "Negroes," or because their
fathers were slaves, but simply because they are not white. This
realization gives an entirely new dimension to the problem and
adds to it international implications of extreme dimensions.
Among other things, it says that the civil-rights fight in the
United States is but one segment of a global battle to take the
profit and the power out of color—or the lack of it.

President Truman saw clearly the growing importance of race
in the formation of foreign policy as far back as 1946 when he
set up a committee to study the problem of civil rights. The
committee's findings left no doubt that the President's concern
was well justified. Its report to the President read in part:

> Our position in the post-war world is so vital to the future that
> our smallest actions have far-reaching effects. We have come to
> know that our own security in a highly interdependent world is
> inextricably tied to the security and well-being of all people and
> all countries. Our foreign policy is designed to make the United
> States an enormous, positive influence for peace and progress
> throughout the world. We have tried to let nothing, not even
> extreme political differences between ourselves and foreign na-
> tions, stand in the way of this goal. *But our domestic civil rights
> shortcomings are a serious obstacle.* [Emphasis, mine] . . . The
> international reason for acting to secure our civil rights now is
> not to win the approval of our totalitarian critics. . . . But we are
> more concerned with the good opinion of the peoples of the
> world. . . . *The United States is not so strong, the final triumph*

*of the democratic ideal is not so inevitable that we can ignore
what the world thinks of our record.*[22]

It is significant that the committee report based its rationale
for wishing to improve the domestic civil-rights situation not on
its own merits, nor upon common justice, but upon the desire
to harvest "the good opinion of the people of the world . . ."
In this effort we have not been altogether successful. Possibly
it is precisely because our motives have been political rather
than humanitarian. Nonwhites abroad know that the spirit of
promotional expedience which motivates "justice" in the United
States today may well be the same spirit which operates in the
highly speculative political arrangements they have frequently
found themselves a party to with the United States. James
Farmer, who was National Director of the Congress of Racial
Equality, reported after a tour of Africa in 1965:

> In the course of my travels, I found that the image of the United
> States in the minds of most of the Africans I met was distinctly
> unfavorable. It was compounded of two factors: reports of the
> American Negro's struggle for freedom in the context of a domi-
> nant white power structure that, to the African, is all too reminis-
> cent of colonial authority; and the effect created by present
> United States policies in Africa.[23]

Farmer adds, gratuitously, that anti-Americanism is increasing
in Africa and that much of the increase is due not solely to
sympathy for the Negro struggle, but is a direct response to our
foreign policy. "It is," he says, "widely believed that the United
States has, for whatever reasons, allied itself with the most reactionary forces in Africa," and this policy is "regarded as divisive
and potentially destructive of African unity. . . . They base their
distrust of the United States on three main aspects of our policy:
our activities in the Congo, our relations with South Africa, and
our relations with Portugal." [24]

Negroes in this country, as well as most Africans (and, doubt-less, many Asians), believe that tacit American support is the key factor in the stability of the government of South Africa and in that country's arrogant suppression of human rights. One reason why the unlamentable passing of the erstwhile Prime Minister Hendrick Verwoerd has raised no new hopes of African freedom in South Africa is that Africans in Africa, like Negroes in the United States, believe firmly that Mr. Verwoerd, and all the Verwoerds who will follow him, was no more than the symbol of the Western white man's intention to maintain at all costs this last outpost of white supremacy.

Vietnam has raised new questions about the possible existence of an international diplomacy in which racial considerations may be decisive. Not many Negroes believe, for example, that the United States and Russia (another white nation) will ever fight each other. On the other hand, it is a common grass roots belief that our policies toward China are, at least in part, racially motivated, and that sometime in the future the United States and Russia will join in a war of elimination against the yellow Chinese. The bombing of Hiroshima rather than of Berlin during World War II is cited widely as de facto evidence of the racial cast of our international policy; the belief persists despite our official protestations that the bomb was "not ready" before the capitulation of Germany.

The war in Vietnam poses a real emotional dilemma for the typical Negro American. His traditional patriotism and his un-willingness to be identified with what to him is "finksmanship" (which he translates as various strategies for avoiding military service) represent opposing values. And although he does not see the Vietnamese problem as being directly related to his problem of racial identity here in the United States, he does have a suspi-cion that he is a pawn in a racial contest which requires him to serve and die in disproportionate numbers fighting a people of whom he'd never heard over an issue he does not understand for a freedom he does not enjoy at home. He remembers with what reluctance Negroes were permitted to fight the Germans in both World Wars, and he suspects that his color is being exploited as a diplomatic asset in a foreign policy anxious to deny that the Vietnam war is a racial contest between whites and nonwhites.

While some of the civil-rights organizations like the NAACP have found it injudicious to associate themselves with the Vietnam peace movement, others like Martin Luther King's Southern Christian Leadership Conference (which can be interpreted as having a moral responsibility) and the Student Nonviolent Coordinating Committee (which has lost most of its white support, anyway) went on record decrying the war in Vietnam.[25]

As the American Negro minority grows more vocal, as it becomes more politically powerful, and as its identification with the struggles of emergent Africa and Asia is strengthened by the mutual recognition of one common problem—*color*, the Negro minority is destined to become an important counterweight to the traditional racial tone which has in the past characterized our foreign policy. This will be well for the future of the United States if we seriously continue to contemplate the leadership and the respect of what is left of the free world.

Professor Arnold Rose correctly observes that in "the present drive to obliterate segregation and discrimination, there is no doubt that one of the catalysts that set the process in motion after World War II was the growing realization in top government circles that discrimination in the United States would hurt, perhaps irreparably should it continue, our fight against Communism." [26] Thus it is that our foreign relations program, or by extension, our inordinate fear of communism, becomes an important liberating factor in the racial struggle at home. It has been said bitterly and often that the Germans (in two world wars) have done more to liberate the American Negro than all of the churches, all of the courts, and all of the "goodwill" in America. If this is true, how ironic would be the prospect of the final liberation coming from the Red Chinese!

## NOTES

1. Mr. Branton is now a member of the Civil Rights Division of the Department of Justice.

2. John Hope Franklin, *From Slavery to Freedom*, 2nd ed. (New York: Alfred A. Knopf, Inc., 1956), p. 127.

3. *Ibid.,* p. 128.

4. Lerone Bennett, Jr., *Before the Mayflower: A History of the Negro in America, 1619–1962* (Chicago: Johnson Publishing Co., 1962), p. 56.

5. Franklin, *op. cit.,* p. 131.

6. *Ibid.,* p. 134.

7. Charles P. Howard, *Freedomways,* Spring 1963, p. 175.

8. *Ibid.,* p. 175.

9. C. Eric Lincoln, *The Black Muslims in America* (Boston: Beacon Press, 1961), p. 59.

10. *Ibid.,* p. 61.

11. *Ibid.*

12. *Ibid.,* p. 63.

13. See Essien-Udom, "The Relationship of Afro-Americans to African Nationalism," *Freedomways,* Fall 1966, p. 391.

14. Rayford Logan, "The Historical Aspects of Pan-Africanism: A Personal Chronicle," *African Forum,* Summer 1965, p. 90.

15. Howard, *op. cit.,* p. 175.

16. Logan, *op. cit.,* p. 94.

17. John A. Davis, "The Influence of Africans on American Culture," *The Annals of the American Academy of Political and Social Science,* 354 (July 1964): 81.

18. American Negro Leadership Conference on Africa, *Resolutions* (Harriman, New York: November 23, 24, 25, 1962).

19. *Ibid.*

20. John Henrik Clark. "The New Afro-American Nationalism," *Freedomways,* Fall 1961, p. 285.

21. "Brotherhood of Blackness," *Negro Digest,* May 1966, p. 5.

22. *To Secure These Rights, The Report of the President's Committee on Civil Rights* (Washington, D.C.: U.S. Government Printing Office, 1947), pp. 146–148.

23. "An American Negro's View of African Unity," *African Forum*, 1, no. 1 (Fall, 1965): 73.

24. *Ibid.*, p. 76.

25. *Freedomways,* Winter 1966, pp. 6, 7.

26. Arnold and Caroline Rose, eds., *Minority Problems* (New York: Harper and Row, 1965).

# 3 Racial Problems and American Foreign Policy

*Paul Seabury*

Most Americans have short memories about their nation's foreign policy. The mass media foreshorten this perspective by focusing heavily on immediate and spectacular current questions, but the habit was not invented by television. It is part of our national character to be present and future-oriented. This habit has both positive and negative sides. Americans are not long on grudges. We may not be very forgiving, but we can be more immediately forgetful. We have trouble in sizing up new situations, often failing to perceive the background against which to place some new occurrence. What is new really seems new. This surely has been the case with what seems to be the recent escalation of race conflicts in the United States to the level of national politics, affecting both our foreign policy and our international relations.

However, in fact multiethnic America frequently has faced foreign policy crises in which domestic race and nationality issues have loomed large. In the Mexican-American War of 1846–1848, large numbers of Irish Catholics actually defected to the other side, choosing as Catholics to defend what they regarded as a Catholic nation. Before World War II, as the political ana-

60

lyst Samuel Lubell has suggested, the social sources of American isolationism and antiwar sentiment were largely ethnic. Times of war, or threatened war, have classically been occasions when issues of race and nationality have most dramatically surfaced to public attention. Sharp cleavages of opinion and attitude have temporarily sundered the American public. Now that we experience a civil-rights "revolution," while engaging the remainder of our attention with a war, we must try to place this problem in a historical perspective.

Race and cultural quarrels are not newcomers to American foreign policy, but until very recently, studies of their effect have been limited only to European, white as opposed to nonwhite, minority influence. Negroes, while greatly studied as a domestic problem, were considered to have shed their African ties soon after they stepped from the slave ships; orientals, Puerto Ricans, Mexican-Americans were insignificant groups unable to influence American foreign policy. The United States was an Atlantic nation. That she practiced economic imperialism in Latin America and acquired an empire in the Pacific was forgotten in the single-minded concentration on European affairs.

Recognizing this yawning gap, but leaving it for another to fill in, let me explore briefly the ways in which European minority groups in the United States have influenced its foreign policy, for even this hypothesis has not always been accepted. Again, until recently, most students of race and ethnic relations in America assumed that domestic racial quarrels stopped at the water's edge. This ethnocentric view considered American race relations primarily in terms of problems that were uniquely American. Comparative sociologists and political scientists are rapidly revising this outlook and have offered theoretical perspectives with which to study the influence of race on foreign policies of all plural societies.

One of the earliest as well as the largest non-Anglo-Saxon Protestant European ethnic groups to arrive in the United States was, of course, the Irish Catholics. In the seven years between 1847 and 1854, 1.2 million Irish were driven from their island home largely by severe economic hardships including the disastrous potato famine of 1848. By the end of the Civil War, Irish people formed 7 percent of the total white population.[1] The percentage decreased somewhat after the waves of Eastern European immigrants during the 1880s.

Irish Catholicism, which has tended to be anti-British, "liberationist," and often chauvinist, has provided a perspective often at odds with dominant American views on foreign policy. Occasionally it converged with such views. Some writers, like the late Louis Adamic, have suggested that the American Revolution relied heavily on this source of radical ethnic zeal, especially in northern seaboard cities. Quoting an English writer, Adamic noted:

> Of the Irish colonists in America, a large proportion everywhere stood foremost on the side of the Patriots. It seemed as if Providence had mysteriously used the victims of British cruelty to Ireland, the men whom her persecution had banished from the bosom of their own land, as the means of her final punishment and humiliation on a foreign soil.[2]

A one-track guideline, Irish opinion has been consistently hostile to U.S. policies congenial to England and vice versa. It was often deaf to more general policy considerations, such as the national security of the United States through alliances. This was so, because for nearly 150 years, Irish independence was entirely an anti-British issue. The now familiar hostility to "imperialism" in American society had its nineteenth-century origins less in Marxism than in County Cork and Dublin, where its most conspicuous West European victims then resided.

Irish opinion exerted itself most strongly during and after World War I. Predictably, it opposed entry into war on the side of the British. Although Irish Catholics could not prevent

American participation in the war, American Anglophiles went so far overboard in their support of the British war effort that Irish nationalists, led by Tammany Judge Daniel F. Cohalan, were able to effectively oppose United States ratification of the Versailles Peace Treaty and the Covenant of the League of Nations. Irish-Americans were particularly opposed to Article X of the Covenant, which guaranteed the territorial integrity of all member states. To them this insured the continued subjugation of Ireland. During 1919–1920 numerous organizations dedicated to Irish independence sprang up in the United States, including the American Association for the Recognition of the Irish Republic, the Irish Self-Determination Club, and the Friends of Irish Freedom.

The isolationist spirit of Irish-America coincided with the rise of the Sinn Fein movement in Ireland, which was largely financed from the United States. The American Commission on Irish Independence appeared at the Versailles peace talks to promote the Irish cause. De Valera, the newly named president of the Irish Republic, escaped mysteriously from his English prison and toured the United States during World War I to arouse the American people against the treaty, later against the League, and for Irish independence. He was extremely successful.

Again, anti-British isolationism was the single motivating factor behind Irish Catholic opinion prior to World War II, and remained a strong force until it was submerged by the patriotic clamor for war after Pearl Harbor.

German-Americans, who constitute the second largest European ethnic group in the United States, have had an effect on American foreign policy similar to that of the Irish. German immigrants came in three waves: prior to the Civil War, between 1865 and 1885, and in the twentieth century after World War I until the early 1950s. The creation of a unified Germany under Bismarck in 1870 spurred public celebrations in many American cities, but unlike the Irish-Americans, German immigrants played no significant part in unification of their homeland. The mid-1880s clash of interests between Germany, the United States, and Britain over the administration of Samoa was the only substantial intervention on the part of German-Americans in American foreign policy during the nineteenth century. According to Louis L. Gerson,[3] their dissatisfaction with the tripartite Samoan settlement contributed significantly to the defeat of Grover Cleveland in the election of 1888.

The Anglophobic coalition with the Irish-Americans began in earnest in 1914 and continued substantially unabated at least until 1941. German-Americans were strongly isolationist and neutralist prior to both world wars. In a study of Woodrow Wilson, Arthur S. Link quotes the president as saying, "We definitely have to be neutral, since otherwise our mixed populations would wage war against each other." [4] In 1941, a U.S. government report showed that German ethnic communities voted in national elections during both wars for the interests of their fatherland, and that 90 percent of the German press in the United States was pro-Nazi. American entry into World War II again muted the divisive tendencies of the German-Americans. But as Lawrence H. Fuchs, in his study of minority groups and American foreign policy, summed up the effects of these two ethnic groups:

> The persistence of chronic German- and Irish-American Anglophobia during the past eighty years has been an important internal factor in the making of American foreign policy. Its total effect has been to stall presidents and secretaries of state in their efforts to implement what they perceived to be a harmony of English and American interests.[5]

While Italian-Americans reacted similarly to German-Americans prior to World War II, immigrants from Eastern Europe—Poland, Russia, Rumania, Czechoslovakia—have generally been strongly interventionist and pro-British. Eastern Europeans were

relatively recent arrivals in America, coming in large numbers
during the 1880s and reaching their peak in 1921. Before and
during World War I, many groups sought to bring U.S. power
to bear against Imperial Germany, Austria, and Russia to liberate their home countries. Similar efforts were made during
World War II and in the cold war, when Stalinist Russia had
overrun Eastern Europe. The "captive nations" constituencies
of recently arrived East Europeans came to represent, during
the height of the cold war, the hard core of U.S. liberationism,
who opposed the containment policy of the Truman administration and supported "roll back" efforts to force a showdown
with Stalin, and establish free governments in Eastern Europe.

The Jewish population in the United States represents a distinct ethnic group. The first immigrants, a handful of Sephardic
refugees from Spanish-Portuguese persecution in Brazil, arrived
in 1654. However, until the nineteenth century, Jews numbered
only a tiny fraction of the total population. They began arriving in great numbers from Germany and Austria, particularly,
in the post-Waterloo period until after the failures of the liberal
1848 revolution. By far the largest group of Jewish immigrants
came from Eastern Europe, Russia, Rumania, and Poland, between 1880 and World War I. In those thirty-five years the
Jewish population, mostly rural peasants, rose to 2.5 million.
Finally, Nazi atrocities in German-held territory precipitated the
most recent influx, estimated around 10,000 annually from the
early 1930s until shortly after World War II. This latest group
was generally more highly educated and middle class than the
earlier arrivals.

As might be guessed, the pattern of Jewish immigration has
influenced their role in American foreign policy matters. Prior
to the nineteenth century, the Jewish population was too insignificant to have any appreciable effect on foreign policy. In fact,
until the early years of the twentieth century, Jewish interest
centered on only two areas of concern: (1) the repeal of dis-

criminatory commercial treaties, (2) treatment of Jews in foreign countries. In both areas Jews were only sporadically successful in making their views felt. In 1840 Van Buren was persuaded to intervene diplomatically in Damascus to protect Jews accused of ritual murder. But in the 1857 "Mortara incident," despite mass meetings held in New York and other U.S. cities, President Buchanan refused to intercede with the Pope on behalf of an Italian boy kidnapped by papal authorities from his Jewish parents.

Similarly, Jews were unable to force a change in a commercial treaty with Switzerland in 1855, which allowed the Swiss to expel American Jews without due process or proper protection for their financial interests. In the 1908 presidential election, the failure of Russia to honor American passports held by Jewish citizens became a campaign issue, but William Howard Taft failed to keep his promise to remedy the situation after his election.

Because of the enormous flood of foreign-born immigrants, Congress, beginning in 1897, tried to impose immigration restrictions, which would require literacy tests and certificates of character from the countries of origin. These bills, which would have effectively eliminated Jewish immigration were vigorously opposed by American Jews, and were successively vetoed by Cleveland, Taft, and Wilson. When Harding finally signed into law the Immigration Act of 1924, the scope of the restrictions had been substantially broadened to include most of the non-northern European minority groups.

The success of Jewish-Americans in influencing foreign policy in the era since World War I has been more fully documented. Their aims have been two-fold: to gather U.S. support for the establishment of the independent state of Israel, and since World War II, to gain admission to the United States for displaced Jews. The groups most concerned with the creation of Israel were the Zionist Organization of America, which numbered

250,000; Hadassah, the women's auxiliary; and the American Zionist Emergency Council, which was responsible for the over-all coordination of various Zionist groups. The major anti-Zionist organization in the United States has been the American Council for Judaism.

Like most minority groups, Jewish-Americans have exerted their influence primarily through the electoral process. During the 1948 presidential campaign, the Jewish community success-fully pressured both political parties to adopt Zionist planks in their party platforms. In a few local elections, with a large Jewish minority, candidates of both parties were forced to outbid each other in their enthusiasm for the new state of Israel, which fre-quently became the major issue in the campaign.

The overwhelming success of the "Jewish" position in recent years on the various Middle East questions has been attributed to the simple fact that there are few Arabs in the United States and quite a large number of Jews.

Throughout the twentieth century, Jewish-Americans have been considerably less isolationist, less military-interventionist, and more liberal in their foreign policy outlook. Jews have more readily supported world government schemes, including the establishment of both the League of Nations and the United Nations, the Marshall Plan for Europe, and foreign aid. As might be expected, however, such support is not uniform within the Jewish population. A recent study of southern Jews, by Alfred Hero, indicates that they are considerably less "Jewish" and more rigidly conservative on foreign policy matters than their northern coreligionlists.[6]

Several generalizations can be made about this historical ex-perience of race and foreign policy in America prior to 1945.

Insofar as racial or nationality questions have arisen in the past to affect judgments on foreign policy crises, they have done so within minority groups which without exception wished to be integrated into American society. The aspirations of European ethnic minorities have almost invariably been assimilationist. By way of contrast, ethnic minorities in many other parts of the world more typically have sought *protection from* the dominant culture, rather than *access to* its values.

In America before World War II, disputes among European ethnic groups about foreign policy invariably were triggered by foreign events over which nationality groups themselves had virtually no control. In this sense, these groups were passive victims of the nationality and nation-state conflicts which tore European society apart in the later nineteenth century, consummated in the racial horror of Hitler's time. Between 1939 and 1941, the locales of powerful isolationist pressures against Roosevelt's intervention policies were those states and regions with Irish and German populations. It should be pointed out, however, that by and large these groups were not pro-Nazi.

Since these European events were a chief source of America's domestic "tribal" tensions, their outcome in 1945 decisively affected subsequent American outlooks on foreign policy. The end of Hitler's Germany signified an enormous defeat for European racist and tribal doctrines. A new Western European ethos after 1945 was integrationist and antiracist. Also, the new threat of Soviet expansion through Central Europe fostered an awareness among European nationality groups of a common threat they heretofore had not perceived. By the beginning of the cold war in 1947, nearly all the classic reasons for American interethnic fighting over foreign policy were gone.

The new controversies in American politics which arose after 1946 paradoxically reversed a previous ethnic situation. In the late 1930s many continental hyphenates in the United States urged us to remain out of Europe's wars. In the late 1940s and early 1950s, the opposite was true—especially of those Central and East European minorities: Poles, Czechs, Slovaks, Slovenes, and others, who now called for an active American policy in Europe—namely for the liberation of their homelands, the "captive nations"—by means of a U.S.-sponsored "rollback." By 1952, groups such as these launched a strong attack against the Truman-Kennan policy of containment, a doctrine which implicitly rejected a push forward in favor of a holding strategy, and thus tacitly recognized the fact of Soviet domination in Eastern Europe.

This phase of the American ethnic disputes over foreign policy ended, for all practical purposes, in the late 1950s. Probably, one could date its end at 1956—the time of the Budapest uprisings, when the terribly high price of U.S. military intervention (i.e., a major war with the Soviet Union) was quite clear.

The classic cold war, however, has had a unique effect on the race factor in the foreign policies of all countries, but most particularly Russia and the United States. At its height there was a close correspondence between military and political-cultural bipolarity in world politics. Russia and America then dominated the realm of strategic power politics; each also commanded its own combination of allies—nations, states, or movements. The principal point of confrontation lay in Europe and the Mediterranean area.

During this fifteen-year period of Soviet-American conflict between 1948 and 1963, certain basic principles of social organization were elevated to an unusually high point. The "issues" involved in their confrontation tended to be universal ones (democracy versus communism, capitalism versus socialism, freedom versus totalitarianism) or realpolitik ones—i.e., a simple power struggle between America and Russia.[7] Yet whether the conflict was "universalist" or "realist," it tended to subordinate greatly themes of race and color. The pot, of course, called the kettle black: Americans have pointed to the fact that the Soviet Union itself has been an "imperialist oppressor" of nationalities within its borders and of nation-states in its satellite areas. The Soviet Union has pointed up imperfections in American society, especially the problem of the American Negro, as instances of "capitalist" oppression.

But what American liberalism and Soviet Marxism both shared, in part by virtue of their common intellectual origins, was a profound rejection of racist doctrines which had previously served to integrate, or disintegrate, European societies. As Marxism—classical or Stalinist—owed its principal philosophical origins in large measure to Enlightenment thought, so its integrative principles were based upon conceptions of social equality not fundamentally different from liberal ones in one crucial respect: their common stress upon human solidarity based upon commonly shared human, not racial, qualities. In this respect, both of them were "true" enemies of racist National Socialism in Europe.[8] Both American liberalism and Soviet Marxism stressed ideas of a future shape of political things in which race and nationality at best would comprise building blocks for more comprehensive multinational groupings of states and movements. (Whatever the differences between political-cultural developments in Eastern and Western Europe after 1947, it certainly is true that Stalinist hegemony over the Eastern nations—Czechoslovakia, Bulgaria, Rumania, and Poland—brought some respite from the furious nationality struggles of the earlier period.)

Nevertheless, the bipolarity of the cold war carried within itself the seeds of its own destruction. Although the confrontation between Soviet Marxism and American liberalism during this period tended to subordinate most other conflict situations in the world, Soviet-American competition in the non-European world on balance tended to hasten greatly the process of European decolonization and successful independence of nonwhite peoples in Asia, Africa, and elsewhere.

The end of the classic cold war can be seen chiefly in the replacement of a condition of relative political bipolarity with one of political multipolarity. America and Russia are still the superpowers in a strategic sense: that is, in their capabilities for waging massive war. But in other respects, especially in their capacity to manage successfully great coalitions, they now have far less influence.

The new world of the post-cold war era is a peculiar one in that some of its more visible characteristics might be said to be retrogressive, in terms of the classical expectations of Western liberalism and of Marxism. Retrogressive *and* "distintegration-ist," one might add. Since the mid-1960s, irrespective of region, the world has been experiencing the revival of ethnic, tribal, and racial tendencies toward apartheid. This can be seen, in Europe, in renewed hostilities between Flemings and Walloons, Welsh and English, Basques and Spaniards, Serbs and Croats, Czechs and Slovaks. In North America, it can be seen in mount-ing tensions between Quebecois and English-speaking Canadians, and in the color crisis in cities in the United States. In Asia, it can be seen in Communist China's sponsorship of "Third World"—movements and ideologies, and in its chauvinist expul-sion of non-Chinese influences from its own territories. In South-east Asia and the Indian subcontinent, the same tendencies are to be seen in clashes between Chinese minorities and dominant majorities of Malays, and in the current crisis of the Indian government to maintain national unity among polyglot subcul-tures. The Middle Eastern crisis between Arab and Jew con-tinues. In Africa, the immense massacres of blacks by Arabs in the Sudan, the Nigerian civil war, and the racial crisis in South-ern Africa bear a bleak witness to the recrudescence of tribalism.

It is not reassuring to note that in the non-Western and non-Communist world attempts by some political leaders to create forms of solidarity among polyglot populations have involved the invocation of neocolonial specters, anti-Western, and in some instances antiwhite ideologies. It certainly is clear that no par-ticular nation—developed or underdeveloped—has a monopoly on these discontents. Western Europe perhaps has been the most immune from them, although the racial tensions in England between new Commonwealth immigrants and "nativists" suggest otherwise.

This international revival of ethnic-racial discontent is conditioned by crosscurrents not explicitly racist. Many followers of Franz Fanon have concluded that there should be an immense "revolt against the West" by long-suppressed proletarian cultures—i.e., an inevitable rebellion against "whites" by "all those others." Suspicious Russians may perceive the old spook of the "yellow peril" more vividly than others. Many guilt-laden intellectuals, both in America and elsewhere, now portray the emerging "crisis" as one between a heartless technological civilization of northern hemispheric nations, and the nontechnocratic, backward nations to the south. A good deal of *mea culpa*, floating around Europe and America both, seeks to blame Western nations for the sorry plight of poverty-stricken, famished, and overpopulated backward nations. But the revival of racism simply cannot be seen as a mere function of economic inequality, "West" versus "Third World," technology versus humanism, or "rich North versus poor South." Another point must be made: these tribal, racial conflicts are modified or held in check in important ways by countervailing influences, including realistic assessments of the prices to be paid, and the horrors to be experienced, from pursuit of tribalist policies. One recoils from the specters of massacres, forced population transfers, and South African pass systems. And yet one somehow continues to believe in the possibilities of human coexistence in freedom under nondiscriminationist systems of constitutional law.

How do such new developments affect the problem of America's relationship to its outside environment? How important today are race, ethnicity, and hyphenate nationality in public attitudes toward America's foreign policies?

The first thing to note is that America is less and less a multiracial society; ethnic tensions among whites today play probably a smaller role than ever before in day-to-day American politics.

America no longer is a nation of immigrants. Even the "Catholic issue" has disappeared. Some intellectuals may deny it, but it is still true that a southern white populist from Texas—Lyndon Johnson—managed to command strong political support even in the North and even among northern Negroes. There is now no particular reason why a Jew or a Negro cannot run on a presidential ticket. The iron law which said that an Irish Catholic could not be elected President turned out to be rather mushy when put to the test in 1960. The foreign policy establishment in Washington, which once was regarded as a special preserve of eastern, white, Protestant, rich, college-educated Anglo-Saxons from Yale, Harvard, and Princeton, has now given way to a complex ethnic melange more distinguished by its expertise than simply by its growing diversity. DeGaulle continued to regard America as an Anglo-Saxon country, conspiring with England to subjugate the Gauls and other more cultivated peoples. But American WASPS would wonder.

So we are now left with the question of the American Negro and American foreign policy. I say it this way, rather than saying the American Negro and the Vietnam war. For, while to many of us the war seems an object of interminable fixation, it would be a mistake to become hypnotized by it, to the exclusion of all other facets of America's international interests, commitments, and purposes. Also, there is no such thing as an endless war. Some day, this one will end. But the problems of the American Negro in American society will go on for a very long time; and these problems will inevitably occur in a larger world context where nonwhite races share, with the American Negro, the problem of poverty in a world of potential abundance and technical productivity. Other issues, crises, and problems will follow Vietnam and command our attention. Civil rights, economic opportunity, and racial discrimination will be with us for quite some time.

It is, however, because the civil-rights revolution and the

Vietnam war accidentally coincide that we should examine their relationship and the symbolic ramifications of both of them at this point in time.

In the past two and a half years, some observers have sought to read into the Vietnam conflict certain cultural and ethnic connotations, whose logic would exist even were there no civil-rights problem in America at all. There have been two principal schools of thought about this, existing in uneasy and inexplicit alliance with each other, and both highly critical of American involvement in this war. Yet the underlying judgments and evaluations of each are markedly different.

A first school of thought, perhaps most explicitly circulated by Walter Lippmann, has sought to convey the impression that what happens in Asia, to Asian peoples, is insignificant; that America is an "Atlantic" nation, and its real ties are with the more advanced countries of Europe. John K. Galbraith, our former Ambassador to India, made a similar point, too, when he remarked in 1966 that Vietnam was, after all, an "insignificant" little country, and hardly worth paying attention to. Real culture, and real affinities, lie elsewhere.

Inversely, others have argued that "white" Americans, or white men generally, have no longer a "right" to be in Asia or, for that matter, in any other nonwhite area of the world. The future of Asia belongs to Asians. The day of the "white man" in these parts of the world is over and gone, just as Rudyard Kipling is gone. This doctrine, a kind of reverse apartheid argument, is frequently shouted by some in the American New Left. Its domestic implications for a so-called white society, where nonwhites—including many Asian-Americans—are a minority, are not mentioned.

Yet whatever else it may be, Vietnam has not been an ethnic war. Both sides are composed of complex coalitions of nations and of ideological movements. On our side, in addition to the multicultural forces of Vietnam opposed to Hanoi's brand of communism, are the United States, New Zealand, Australia, Thailand, the royalists and neutralists of Laos, the Philippines, and South Korea. Material support comes from many other countries of Asia and Europe. On the "other side," are the Vietcong, the North Vietnamese government, aided by China, the Soviet Union, "white" East European communist regimes, and many other communist movements. It should be clear that Vietnam cannot simply be seen either as a racial war or as an "Asian" war. It has been a civil war within an Asian country, with widely recognized international implications for the delicate balance between the communist world and ours. The civil war aspect long since has been overridden by the international one, and this is *not* an ethnic one.

While the basis of the Vietnam conflict is not racial, it is not entirely accidental that the war should coincide with heightened race problems in the United States. These are immensely complex events, with more than one point of conjuncture and interaction. Looking at the economic effects of the war on the so-called war on poverty, one immediately notes at least two contradictory effects. Vietnam has occasioned, and certainly served as excuse for, substantial cuts in federal antipoverty programs. But since American wars characteristically have hastened the pace of racial integration, Vietnam is not necessarily an exception to this rule. It *is* true that proportionately more American Negroes than white are now serving in the war. But—regardless of the complex moral issue of inequity which this poses—this in itself as in the past will probably hasten, rather than retard, the process of ethnic integration by serving as a surrogate college education for the economically deprived.

Looking at the political interrelationships between Vietnam and the civil-rights movement, one can also see contradictory patterns. It is true that the war has been an occasion for extremist racist groups to exploit dissatisfactions. It has given Black Power devotees and even more fanatical sects a chance to link demagogically their separatist causes to a larger issue. No doubt some racist ideologues see the Negro ghetto as only one of many battlegrounds of struggle against "Washington imperialism." Some moderate civil-rights leaders have drawn quite different implications from both theaters; convinced as they have been of the moral authority of nonviolent action, they have logically—if unrealistically—sought to apply their own norms of social action to the Vietnam conflict. Finally, the style of disobedience, applied with such success to resist illegal and unconstitutional white racist authorities in the South and else-where, has spilled over into the larger theater of national politics and foreign policy as a multipurpose if dangerous device for redressing any grievance, real or fancied, and any law, con-stitutional or otherwise.[9] The style and tactic no longer are con-fined to legitimate ethnic issues and grievances, or for that matter to specifically ethnic issues.

Yet at the same time, we note contradictory evidence: for, as opinion polls have pointed out since 1965, the popularity of the Johnson Administration among American Negroes *as a whole* was not significantly different than among other Ameri-cans. At times, during the Vietnam war, it was in fact even higher. More Negroes than whites, furthermore, support the Vietnamese war (though it should be pointed out that among college-educated Negroes, the rate of dissent appears slightly higher than among their white equivalents).

The reason for this may not be hard to find, nor surprising. The Vietnam war coincided with the greatest legislative break-through on civil rights and racial equality in American history. American Negroes would certainly have been peculiar if they had responded toward the Johnson administration in any dif-ferent fashion than they did. Much of the racial violence in American cities may be due to the disparity between expecta-tion and fulfillment, and between administration promises and existing realities. But if we read the polls correctly, American

Negroes rate the domestic issue of equality of opportunity far higher than they rate the importance of Vietnam, one way or another. There probably is no higher proportion of idealists among Negroes than in other parts of American society; but I would hazard the guess that there are substantial numbers of realists among them.

The marathon Arab-Israeli war among other things reminds us that the world of international politics contains many other risks than Vietnam. So, too, our own preoccupation with this particular conflict should make us aware that there most certainly are more limited wars in our future. This is not the last generation which will run the risk of involvement in collective violence for some purpose or other. If this is a reasonable guess, we must now ask: how may America's "racial politics" gear into future features of our foreign policy?

An apartheid America, in a world of other racial strains and stresses, will be unable to participate effectively and constructively in an international community. An America which persists towards closer integration and equality of opportunity regardless of race, religion, or color, will remain what it has been until now: something of an example to others. On the other hand, an America sharply divided between blacks and others will be a disastrous example to other nations, just as once, a generation or so ago, American successes in "solving" its ethnic problems among its European nationalities served as a positive and constructive example to Europe.

Looking only at our past successes in foreign policy, they have, on the whole, been ones which came from acting in close constructive tasks with wide groupings of other nations. America's effectiveness in such enterprises has sprung not simply from the abundance of the resources we had to put in them, nor from the credibility of the promises and commitments we made. It also has depended upon our "openness" and willingness to tolerate, even encourage, diversity—and on our credible reputation as a "nation of nations" which had richly incorporated in itself *more* foreign influences than perhaps any other major country has ever done. In a world which everywhere shows new signs of revived racial stresses and tensions, an American failure would have not only deep consequences for ourselves, but for the future of open societies in general. In retrospect, this crisis has far greater import than the European ethnic crises which America once experienced in a world which once was, but now is not, run by whites.

## NOTES

1. Peter Rose, *They and We* (New York: Random House, 1964), p. 30.

2. Louis Adamic, *A Nation of Nations* (New York: Harper and Bros., 1944), p. 324.

3. Louis L. Gerson, *The Hyphenate in Recent American Politics* (Lawrence: University of Kansas Press, 1964), p. 51.

4. *Ibid.*

5. Lawrence H. Fuchs, "Minority Groups and Foreign Policy," in *American Ethnic Politics* (New York: Harper and Row), p. 150.

6. Alfred O. Hero, Jr., "Southern Jews, Race Relations, and Foreign Policy," *Jewish Social Studies,* 27 (October 1965): 213–235.

7. See my *Rise and Decline of the Cold War* (New York: Basic Books, 1967).

8. One should not flatter Stalinist Russia too much: after all, the mortal victims of Stalinism, "traitors" and "class enemies," vastly outnumbered Hitler's "racist" victims. A Benthamite might wonder whether it is more pleasurable to perish in consequence of genocide or "classicide."

9. But peace marches in American cities significantly have had very few Negroes in them; neither have the "patriotic" parades.

# 4 | The Civil-Rights Movement and American Foreign Policy

*James A. Moss*

I would like to start out with two assumptions.

American foreign policy, where it touches upon nonwhite peoples in the world, has been singularly marked by "white imperialism" viewed in political terms and "benevolent racism" viewed in ethnic terms. The Boxer Rebellion, our Chinese and Japanese Exclusion Acts, our ready willingness to defend militarily the free world against communist aggression in North Korea and Vietnam; but our *not* so ready willingness to assume this posture in 1961 against East Germany and, most recently, against communist forces in Czechoslovakia, are cases in point.

Our racial double standard was reflected also during World War II, in the internment of Nisei, but not citizens of German descent. One questions also our strong drive to interfere in the internal affairs of Cuba and the Dominican Republic but our silent acquiescence to military tyranny in Argentina and Chile.

Our indefensible economic support of the racist regimes in Rhodesia and South Africa adds substance to what many would deny. Perhaps these examples point up my selective and even distorted perceptions; nevertheless they call for answers. Our foreign policy posture is alarmingly colored by the racial complexion of the countries with which we are involved. We do, indeed, have a bipartisan racial and ethnic foreign policy; one which operates positively toward countries most similar to us—predominantly white, and another which operates negatively for countries whose inhabitants are predominantly nonwhite.

A second assumption argued in this chapter is that America's view of the world suffers from an exaggerated conception of order, defined in terms of a peculiarly unique national character. We pride ourselves on our youth, on our capacity to respond to innovation and rapid change, and on our racial and ethnic diversity. Since we associate these attributes with our position of political, military, and economic strength, we tend to think our way of life is ideal for the less powerful nations in this world.

Order in the world is associated with such values as the free enterprise capitalist system vis-à-vis socialist economic structures; two party forms of government vis-à-vis one party states; national security through military alliances vis-à-vis international organization. Since these highly valued attributes most accurately describe countries in the predominantly white Western world, it follows that Africa, Asia, Latin America, and most of the Far East are areas of the world which represent in our view the greatest threat of instability and conflict with our interests.

An understanding of the efforts of minority groups, particularly nonwhite minority groups, to achieve full citizenship rights in the United States, requires some discussion of the relationship between power and powerlessness. Power is a centrifugal force that propels human beings into roles where they are believed to have or, indeed, do possess the right to influence or make decisions over the lives of others.[1] Power can be absolute or relative, concentrated or diffused, benign or despotic, disguised or blatant. Despite the form it takes, however, it is the salient characteristic that divides groups into "haves and have-nots," into "pariahs" and "chosen people," into inferior and superior castes, and into subordinate and superordinate classes.

While I would hold that what I have to say applies conceptually to all nonwhite minority groups in the United States—and by inference, defines the relationship between the United States and nonwhite societies throughout the world—the major thrust of my remarks applies to the status of black people in America.

Diagrammatically, for purposes of representation, we may conceive of power/powerlessness as a behavioral "field," lying on a horizontal plane $P\text{-} \underline{\hspace{5cm}} P$.

Powerlessness                    Power

Whether the symbolic representation of this "field" is a straight line or a circle, the quantum of power within that "field" is a constant.

Blacks in the United States are represented as the vertical axis (A) along the power continuum $(P\text{-}, P)$ available to all groups at any given moment or period of time. If the reality situation of the black man $(A, A_1)$ in the United States has been, and is, one of almost absolute powerlessness $(P\text{-})$ relative to the total society $(P\text{-}, P)$ then his life chances have been measured by the degree to which he has successfully been able to reduce the amount of power at the disposal of white society $(C, C_1)$ and employ such gains in his own defense. (See Figure 4–1.)

The harsh reality and the harsh truth is that such black power which can be mobilized to free the black man as a

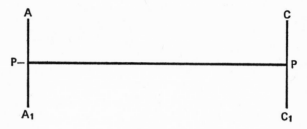

**Figure  4–1**

citizen must be acquired at the expense of white power. (See Figure 4–2.)

I need not belabor the point that American white power in all of its dimensions would be nonexistent today had it not been secured at the expense of imported and exploited black labor. Thus the struggle of Negroes for full citizenship revolves around the potentiality for achieving a just equilibrium (point B) between black powerlessness and white power. (See Figure 4–3.)

In short, if one is white and is powerless in our society, the scale still weighs more favorably for him than for a black. It is certain that his powerlessness is not a function of his whiteness. For the black, however, the overwhelming barrier

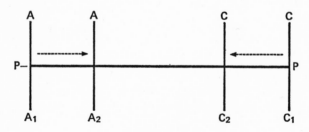

**Figure  4–2**

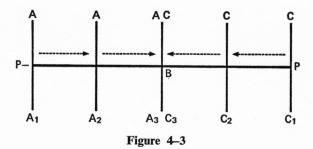

**Figure 4-3**

to his quest for power is the color of his skin—all other things are added to it.[2]

The threat to our society then is not the increasingly growing demands for black power by our militants, but the increased white resistance to legitimate black demands for power and control over decisions that affect their lives directly. A dramatic change in the rhetoric and the commitment to democracy is called for if the growing alienation of blacks from American white society is to be arrested or redirected. The concept of ethnic integration and assimilation has to be replaced by Ruth Benedict's familiar concept of cultural autonomy. White resistance to even token shared black power has to yield to the acceptance of blacks as fully inclusive members in a truly pluralistic, democratic America. I think this is what the civil-rights struggle in the United States has been about. For while I believe there have been some modifications in our domestic racial policies over time, I think the changes wrought have affected more the form of our behavior than the content of our racial ideologies.

For example, the kind of schools blacks attend have undergone changes, but the content of the education they receive remains the same. The quality of housing has improved for blacks, but cultural isolation still marks the lives of most black people. The income of blacks has risen, but entry into higher level skills and professions is almost as remote as ever. Proportionately more blacks live who are born now, but proportionately larger numbers than whites die in almost every health category—to say nothing about homocide and war.[3] In summary, United States racial problems have been and are deeply imbedded in color consciousness and color caste. Racism based upon color differences has been an incipient, if not indigenous, characteristic of our country since its founding. The romantic saga of Captain John Rolfe and Pocahontas is a far cry from the subsequent life experiences of America's largest and most disenfranchised ethnic minority—the American Indian. The ancestors of the more than 500,000 blacks who survived the voyages from Africa still seek the "Promised Land of Freedom" and unrestricted opportunity. Mutiny aboard ship, unremitting slave rebellions, an underground railroad to the North and Canada, experiments with resettlement in Africa, sit-ins, riots, and alternative present-day schemes for repatriation into black communities in this country and outside, all mark unrelenting efforts on the part of black Americans to find some way out. Almost every black child and adult knows in *his* heart that if *he is* to be free in America, *he* must extract that freedom inch by inch from an adversary most adept at retaining *his* power prerogatives almost intact and, until recently, most successful in deluding Negro Americans into believing that they are on the road to racial integration.

The civil-rights struggle of Negroes in the United States documents the seeming futility of the black man's hope for freedom in America. As the largest number of nonimmigrant people in the United States we have sustained physical, emotional, and moral hardships over a longer period of time than any other major population group in a professedly democratic society.

Of all our ethnic groups, it has been blacks who have required continuous legislative support in order to gain access to privileges which accrued naturally to other peoples who arrived at the same time or subsequently on our shores.

In most countries of Latin America and the Caribbean, slaves had been freed by the time formal emancipation decrees were signed or issued. Only in America was it necessary to engage in a major civil war so that black men could be free. The events which chronicle the "fixing of place" of Negroes in American society are too numerous to detail here, but I will cite some of the major points along the way.

The post-Reconstruction period served notice to Negroes that while constitutionally they were free, individually they were still slaves.[4] *Plessy* v. *Ferguson* legally confirmed the permanent inferior status of black people in the United States.[5] A series of failures of black people to escape to freedom in Africa led to a concentration of organized efforts to improve the status of Negroes within the United States. The National Association for the Advancement of Colored People, the National Urban League, the black church, the black press, black schools, and black mutual-aid societies all arose in defense against the unremitting efforts of a powerful white society to maintain black people in a subordinate status in this country. Negroes did not remove themselves from the mainstream of American society into segregated institutions. They were physically and legally pushed out.[6]

It took legal action by the NAACP, in almost every instance, to decide where a black man could live, work, vote, go to school, or travel. Where a black man could eat, sleep, or play, had to await another battlefront.[7] Meanwhile, some Negroes began to look away from the "melting pot" into the reality of expanding, deteriorating, and depressing black ghettos, and into the reality of certain common experiences shared by black men everywhere in the world. A series of Pan-African congresses, a cross fertilization of ideas and experiences by blacks in the West Indies, Africa, and the United States, soon laid the foundation for a black nationalist movement that had to arise not only within the United States, but wherever black men were still held in bondage.[8]

Heightened aspirations were raised for American Negro citizens with the 1954 decision on the schools, only to be shattered by the reality of only 1 percent of black children in desegregated schools ten years after the decree.[9]

An African continent rapidly moving toward independence in 1960 had made the perceived conditions of black men in the United States even less tolerable. "All Africa will be free, before black men in America can even buy a cup of coffee," was an all too bitter complaint of Negro citizens. If it was difficult for white Americans traveling abroad to defend American treatment of Negroes, it was even more humiliating for Negroes to justify or explain their second-class citizenship to people in other countries. Freedom rides, sit-ins, wade-ins, all were signaling a change in the mood of Negroes. Blacks wanted "all the way in" American society; barring this, they wanted out.

Building upon the theme of race pride and black identity eloquently articulated by W. E. B. DuBois, Edward Wilmot Blyden, George Padmore, and Marcus Garvey, the search for black unity began to take on increasingly broader international dimensions. Out of the conference of black writers meeting in Paris under the leadership of Leopold Senghor and others evolved the first articulation of the concept of negritude. Negritude—the expressed appreciation of the cultural, physical, and ideological unity common to black men everywhere—provided at least one of the touchstones for the emergence of black nationalism on an international scale.[10]

If one reads black literature over the last ten years, it is almost impossible to localize the black struggle to a single country or continent. (*The African Presence*—proceedings from the conference of Negro writers in Paris, Richard Wright's *Black Power*, Franz Fanon's *Black Skin, White Masks*, James Baldwin's *Nobody Knows My Name*, Harold Cruse's *The Crisis of the Negro Intellectual*, etc.). Nor is it possible to separate black protest movements in the United States from a sentiment favorable to an identity with black experience in other countries. This is the deepest significance of the trek of almost every major civil-rights leader in the United States, youth or adult, to Africa at some point in their active careers. Indeed, the broader conceptualization of the race struggle to include parts of the world outside the United States has often been attributed to inspiration and insight gained by civil-rights leaders as a consequence of their exposure to Africa.

I think too it is in this renewed search for identity with black brothers elsewhere wherein lies the insistence on the part of major segments of black youth that visible identity with Africa be affirmed through dress, language, political ideology, and, for some, residential preference. While some black organizations assign greater emphasis to the historical relationship of black men to black Africa—American Society for African Culture, the Black Muslims, The Republic of Black Africa, The Student Nonviolent Coordinating Committee, the Black Panthers, etc.—all give at least nominal acquiescence and support to the concept of an international black community.

A combination of circumstances has produced what I would consider one of the significant developments in the contemporary period. I refer here to the organizational thrust of the young black intellectual revolutionary. I suspect I may hit wide of the mark in a few places in this profile, but this is what is coming through to me about and from them. These young people come neither from the hard-core slums, although many live in the ghettos; nor do they come exclusively from the talented 3 percent of the black college-bound. They are the children of black families of modest incomes who have not been whipped into defeat by the system, nor enticed by the promise of success within it. Not a few of them come from families where both parents have achieved success economically and professionally. These young people form the backbone of the black student movements on college campuses across the country. They see themselves as sharing with all of their black brothers in this country educational experience for developing and sustaining a healthy and positive self-conception necessary for survival and productivity in a white-dominated society. Thus, black college students are joining hands with their brothers and sisters in Upward Bound programs, special admissions programs for disadvantaged students on predominantly white campuses, militant organizations of noncollege oriented black youth, and with black youth on predominantly Negro campuses in the South. They are imbuing their younger and less well-educated brothers and sisters with a pride in their African cultural heritage and the long-neglected indigenous black American cultural values and strengths. The black studies programs which are arising on many college campuses, mainly through their insistence and initiative, serve as cultural and educational vehicles for linking past and present aspirations of the American Negro with those of black people in Africa and the Caribbean.

They are dramatizing the failure of American intellectual and cultural institutions to take cognizance of the often unique but ignored contributions of blacks in these institutions. Hardly any recent professional association meeting of significance to black people—Africans, Latin Americans, Caribbeans, Afro-Americans—has not been challenged to address itself to issues directly relevant to the black experience. Where the professional organizations have not already done so, they are being called upon to assure blacks more than a token role in association policy and decision-making, and to seek aggressively larger black representation in their memberships. Black caucuses within the American Sociological Society, the African Studies Association, National Association of Social Workers, black Catholic clergy, etc., are only a few of the organizations so affected.

As the sociologist and historian look back upon the relative ease with which successive waves of white immigrants have been assimilated into the mainstream of American life, they are confronted with the *fact* of the nonassimilation of American blacks. The denial of the American dream to Negroes has forced them, in the interest of their own survival, to look outside our society for psychic support and positive role identification. We have never been accepted members of American society and few of us really believe in its possibility.

In another paper Hugh Smythe and I have summarized the national image of the Negro as follows:

> Despite racial advances, the picture of the Negro remains, historically and traditionally, that of a person looked down on by the majority of white group members, especially the white Anglo-Saxon Protestant, as inferior and occupying an insecure position in the economic organization. The Negro, restricted to education in a predominantly segregated school system, lacking any real force, influence, or authority in the national political structure, possesses a personality marked by oppression, crippled by feelings of inferiority and frustration, and distorted by anger toward whites who seek to enhance their own social status, through support of beliefs in white supremacy, and through preventing the Negro's full participation and action in the mainstream of American life.[11]

Since that writing, a new administration has assumed leadership without a single black in a key national post. On the international diplomatic scene, we have dropped from six black ambassadors, two in Europe and four in Africa, to four: one in Europe and three in Africa. Although there has been a small increase in the number of Negroes entering the foreign service at the junior level, promotion to the top three grades is at a standstill, with less than a dozen senior officers based in Washington or abroad.[12] Yet in the face of mounting domestic racial tension, no major study of the impact of our racial practices at home upon our external relations with other countries has been undertaken by any of our agencies with overseas missions.

I was reminded of our blindness to the corrosive and destructive consequences of our racial ills for our foreign relations, particularly with the darker nations abroad (and certainly not left unexploited by the predominantly white communist countries in Eastern Europe), as I watched an exterminator at work in a house where I was staying recently in the Caribbean. It seemed so easy to ignore the small canals marking the presence of termites attacking the wooden portions of the house. They seemed so insignificant as compared with the size of the building they were attacking, and yet to ignore them would imperil the very foundation of the entire structure. We seem not the least sensitive to the need for preventive maintenance in coping with our national and international racial and ethnic problems. We recognize the danger signals but appear too paralyzed or indifferent to act. Meanwhile, racism continues to eat away at the very foundation of our society, threatening the stability of our national life and causing irreparable damage to our prestige and influence abroad. To those who would ask what we must do to alter our present course of racial behavior, I offer first the completely nonintellectual, unsophisticated answer given to this same question by a black freshman student to my all-white minorities class, "You know what you need to do, stop doing what you're doing. Stop treating us like Niggers!"

I suppose some effort ought to be made to suggest approaches more in keeping with the objectives of this essay.

I should like to propose a necessary step to be taken if we would postpone, if not prevent, a racial holocaust in this country and in other racist countries in the world.

I think we ought to expand substantially our efforts through research, legislation, and programmatic action, to understand the nature, extent, and consequences of racism for the survival of human societies and humankind. Domestically, we ought to face the fact of the intensity of anger and rage that exists within the black community and immediately take the necessary steps to assuage it. The anger of blacks is long standing and deep-cutting. From before the Civil War to the present, the indignities suffered by black men at the hands of white Americans have led black men to seek to separate physically from the United States into a more receptive, hospitable environment. In 1788, Free Negroes considered returning to Africa, and in 1815, Paul Cuffee, an American Negro shipbuilder, sailed to Sierra Leone with thirty-eight Free Negroes. Later, in 1822, Liberia was founded by Africans freed from slavery in America. Then too, Martin Delany, in 1850, explored the possibilities of repatriation of American Negroes into present-day Nigeria. Finally, Marcus Garvey's "Back-to-Africa" movement in the 1920's sought to relocate masses of Negroes from the United States to Africa. All of these efforts eloquently attest to the long-standing disillusionment and disenchantment of blacks in all social strata with the subordinate status historically imposed upon them in this country.[13]

Present-day variants of these past efforts at separation include the expanding landholdings of the Black Muslims and the organization of The Republic of New Africa. Thus, black people have long been angry in America, and abatement of this anger is not yet in sight. Grier and Cobbs write:

> And of the things that need knowing, none is more important than that all blacks are angry. White Americans seem not to

recognize it. They seem to think that all the trouble is caused by only a few "extremists." They ought to know better.[14]

They conclude, "If racist hostility is to subside, and if we are to avoid open conflict on a national scale, information is the most desperately needed commodity of our time." [15]

The kinds of information that we need to have, in the interest of formulating sound policies and practices in American race relations, includes answers to such questions as: Can we determine objectively or measure the will of white Americans to abandon their long-held racial beliefs and practices in support of the full integration of black men into the United States? Much of what is being said and done suggests that it is already too late to talk of integration—the mood is shifting heavily in the black community towards separation. Is it too late even to research the possibilities of black-white rapprochement in the United States? If it is, then one observer cautions us:

> The white American is going to have to let go of his black brother; give him massive economic support, technical advice, scholarships, but leave him to make his own mistakes, learn his own lessons. Nor does he want belatedly offered white friendship—yet. He needs to find his own identity, reconstruct his own past, before he is psychologically free to meet the white man on an equal footing.[16]

The imperative for reexamining our long-held stereotypical image of the black man in America is almost plaintively pointed up by Senator Fred Harris in his introduction to *Black Rage*:

> The answer is clear, yet terribly difficult for most of us to see— that the civilization that tolerated slavery dropped its slaveholding cloak but the inner feelings remained . . . [that] the practice of slavery stopped over a hundred years ago, *but the minds of our citizens have never been freed.*[17]

But it is precisely because institutionalized racism in America is so difficult to see and to admit that our best efforts in research, mass media utilization, and program development constitute a national requirement of the highest priority. Our willingness to commit our human and financial resources to the task should at least equal our national expenditures for defense against cancer or our defense against international communism. Some foci that might well constitute an allout attack on racism in the United States could include:

1. An interpretation of existing research findings on racism, drawing heavily upon the U.S. experience, but not limited to this source

2. A consolidation of documented instances of institutionalized racism in the United States to be used in developing a functional definition of racism for empirically assessing its major currents in the United States

3. Exploration of the range of strategies and alternatives —organizational and individual—necessary to deal effectively with the various forms of racism in the United States

4. Study of the range of countervailing mechanisms employed by majority groups to sustain and reinforce racist practices in the United States

Conceptually, new paradigms for researching U.S. race relations, constructed from base-line data emanating from within the black community, need to complement, if not replace, outdated concepts no longer relevant to the black experience. White researchers need to begin to look into black communities as closely as they can through the eyes of blacks in order to revalidate previous formulations based upon skewed or inaccurate data.

Internationally, also, the United States, and the West, must

begin to deal with the reality of a worldwide community of
nonwhite peoples bound together in a common struggle against
white racism and imperialism in which the United States is
the major protagonist.

The gravity of race as a U.S. domestic problem and as an
international crisis is summarized in a recent statement of the
Institute of Race Relations in London:

> It is no longer necessary to emphasize the importance of race as
> a domestic issue in the United States. In Britain, too, this has
> become a national issue; we may still be in time to learn from
> American experience and prevent the problem reaching the
> gravity it has in the United States, but only if exchange of ideas
> is urgently sought and quickly translated into action.
>
> It is less generally recognised that ideas about race play a part
> in every major confrontation of the world today. World poverty,
> world hunger, world population, and the operation of aid pro-
> grammes, are all affected; efforts for peace, the activities of the
> United Nations, the working of international agencies are frus-
> trated by the suspicions and resentments which arise from race.
> Failures to solve the domestic problem in the United States and
> Britain; failure to enforce the views of the United Nations in
> South West Africa and in Rhodesia, failure to achieve peace in
> Viet-Nam—all increase the sense of frustration among the devel-
> oping nations. The line between rich nations and poor and the line
> between white and non-white are dangerously near coinciding
> and the polarisation of the world into camps divided by these
> lines becomes increasingly serious. In the power struggle between
> the United States, Russia and China, political use is made of this
> polarisation and it is a major contribution to instability. There
> are influential people who speak of a "race war" on a world scale
> as inevitable if not already in progress. But surely more reason-
> able courses are open if men apply their minds to the possibili-
> ties.[18]

The linkages between disaffected blacks in the United States
and their nonwhite allies elsewhere are at least suggested by

reference to a few instances involving nonwhite peoples in
Asia, the Caribbean, and Africa.

Ann Forrester reports that:

> . . . well before the United States' current involvement in Viet
> Nam, black men, meeting in 1945 at the fifth Pan-African Con-
> gress, sent President Ho Chi Minh greetings, assuring him of
> their support in the Viet-minh's struggle against French imperial
> rule.[19]

It seems almost ludicrous to examine Ho Chi Minh's attitude
toward the United States; but when his second in command was
asked, in an interview reported in *Look* magazine, about his
country's postwar economic plans, he replied:

> We will rebuild our nation with the help of our friends. We will
> invite technicians and scientists to come to Vietnam like mis-
> sionaries! and what a beautiful and noble mission! and we de-
> serve it! [20]

When asked whether North Vietnam would invite U.S. economic cooperation and trade, the reply given was: "We are not
vindictive . . . but you have asked a difficult question." [21]

In my recent visit to Kingston, Jamaica, a university professor, born in Trinidad, explained Trinidad's refusal to promote tourism:

> We feel that most American tourists who would come would
> bring their racial prejudices with them. We stand more to lose in
> human relations than we would ever gain in dollars and cents.

Another complaint heard frequently during my stay in the
West Indies was directed at the intellectual imperialism of
North American white universities. Criticism revolved around
the saturation by white institutions of the University of the

West Indies' research resources and facilities without acknowledging on a partnership basis the contributions made by the host country or sharing with the University of the West Indies either the final research product or credit for making the effort successful.

When I visited Puerto Rico recently to explore the possibilities of joint research and faculty exchange between the University of Puerto Rico and the State University of New York at Buffalo, a university official asked, "What do you want to do with us—destroy our identity as Puerto Ricans and make us North Americans? The best thing you can do for us is to close down the branch here, and leave us to ourselves."

In spite of the long tradition of African students studying in the United States, the almost uniform finding of studies conducted with this population reveals that most African students experience some form of racial discrimination during their stay here. Indeed, with one group of African students studying in the Midwest, the longer they stayed, the more disaffected they became. When we consider the history of discrimination toward African diplomats and other distinguished visitors during their stay in this country, coupled with the documented evidence that some of the most damaging effects upon our American-African relations derive from experiences with racially and culturally unsophisticated white Americans on varying assignments in Africa, is it any wonder that we are so disliked in Africa? Joseph Kennedy's research findings five years ago are just as relevant today as then:

> Today, the entire world is caught up in a great two-pronged struggle—a struggle for material and human equality. The American Negro quest for civil rights, the independence of nations, world revolutions, are a part of this larger struggle. For most countries the dissolution of old alliances and the formation of new friendships and relations will be determined by the outcome of this

great struggle. Where this struggle takes on racial overtones, as it must in Africa, (for the African, as the American Negro, has lived with minority status within the concept of white superiority and black inferiority) the United States finds itself in an extremely sensitive, tenuous position—much more so than the Soviet Union or England, or any other country in the world. The United States is the major force in the "free world" standing for democracy, individual expression, and human rights. The United States has the largest black population of any place in the world outside Africa itself. Yet, the United States has an extremely negative racial image in Africa and around the world. The United States also has the greatest racial strife any place in the world outside South Africa.[22]

If America is to alter the image of herself as one of the most hated nations in the world by nonwhite peoples, nothing short of a major transformation in her racial posture and priorities for international action will suffice.

Pastor Martin Niemoller is reported to have made this comment about the societal tendency to set priorities not on the seriousness of the problem to be treated, but on the number of people affected by a social problem:

When labor came to me for help against Hitler, I was silent, because I was not a laborer. When the Jews came to me, I was silent because I was not a Jew. When Catholics came to me, I remained silent because I was not a Catholic, but when the Protestant Church was attacked, I looked around and there was no help to be found.

It would be a pity if the United States, by its continued relegating of nonwhite peoples to positions of ignominy, shame, and insignificance, should at a critical point in its own survival, find itself isolated and alone. Where then shall we turn? What then will be our options? How impregnable will our white defenses be? These are the real questions.

**NOTES**

1. For an excellent treatment of the concept of power as it applies to the dynamics of race relations, cf. Kenneth Clark, "Problems of Power and Social Change," The Kurt Lewin Memorial Award Lecture Society for the Psychological Study of Social Issues, 1965.

2. "The black experience teaches the black that in this democracy the dominant value is majority rule . . . And in a society which values majority rule the predicate for participation is the pigmentation of one's skin." Jesse Nash, Director of Buffalo Model Cities Program. Quoted in the *Buffalo Evening News,* January 30, 1969.

3. U. S. Department of Labor, Bureau of Labor Statistics, *The Negroes in the United States,* Bulletin No. 1511, June 1966.

4. W. E. B. DuBois, *Black Reconstruction* (New York: Harcourt, Brace and Co., 1935). Still one of the best historical treatments of the period.

5. John Hope Franklin, *From Slavery to Freedom* (New York: Alfred A. Knopf, Inc., 1956). Details the systematic resegregation process of blacks after the Reconstruction.

6. *Ibid.*

7. A recently published chronicle of the history of black protest movements in the United States is Benjamin Muse, *The American Negro Revolution* (Bloomington: Indiana University Press, 1968).

8. Selected essays historically tracing the events antecedent to the formal enunciation of the Black Power doctrine in the United States are included in Floyd C. Barbour, ed., *The Black Power Revolt* (Boston: Sargent, 1968).

9. Kenneth Clark, *Dark Ghetto* (New York: Harper & Row, 1965). Victor H. Bernstein, "Why Negroes Are Still Angry," *Redbook,* July 1966. Eighty-four percent of Negroes still attend segregated schools in the South and in the North; more schools are now segregated than there were ten years ago.

10. See Hollis Lynch, "Pan-Negro Nationalism in the New World," *Boston University Paper on Africa,* vol. 2, ed., J. Butler (Boston: Boston University Press, 1966), and Anne Forrester, "Pan-African Activism in the 20th Century." The latter is a chapter in a forthcoming book entitled *The Black Man in America: the Need for Dialogue,* edited by James A. Moss, to be published by the

American Humanist Association. Horace Mann Bond, "The Relations between American Negroes, African Students in the United States, and Africans" (paper read at the National Conference, American Negro Leadership Conference on Africa, Washington, D.C., September 24–27, 1964).

11. Hugh H. Smythe and James A. Moss, "Racial Images Abroad and Making U. S. Foreign Policy" (paper presented to the Conference on Racial Problems in American Foreign Policy, University of Denver, Vail, Colorado, July 1967), p. 4.

12. Idris Rossell, "Equal Employment Opportunity—Too Much or Not Enough?" Reprint, *Foreign Service Journal,* January 1969.

13. Lynch, *op. cit.*; Bond, *op. cit.*

14. Grier and Cobbs, *Black Rage* (New York: Basic Books, Inc., 1968), p. 4.

15. *Ibid.*

16. *Look Magazine,* January 7, 1969, p. 16.

17. Grier and Cobbs, *op. cit.*, p. vii, viii.

18. Draft Submission to the Ford Foundation, Research in Race Relations: an International Unit, The Institute of Race Relations, London, England, 1968, p. 1.

19. Forrester, *op. cit.*, p. 6.

20. *Look Magazine,* January 21, 1969, p. 30.

21. *Ibid.*

22. Joseph C. Kennedy, "Image of the American Negro in Africa" (paper read at the Second National Conference, The American Negro Leadership Conference on Africa, September 1964), pp. 17–18.

# 5 | Race Relations and United States Policy in Asia

*Robert A. Scalapino*

A few years ago I was in the city of Alma Ata, Central Asia, in the far east of the Soviet Union about eighty miles by air from China. I sat down at a restaurant table when two young Kazakhs joined me. They were students at the University of Alma Ata. Kazakhs by racial background are related to the Mongols. These young men, having sat down, noticed that I was a foreigner. They first thought to leave, but then became curious, so we tried to converse. They spoke no English and only a few words of German. I spoke no Russian, and needless to say, no Kazakh. After the "Me Berkeley, you Alma Ata" business, we were about finished when I thought of a game we might play in sign language. Someone mentioned a name like Khrushchev or Stalin, and if you liked him it was thumbs up, if you didn't like him it was thumbs down, and if it was in between, sort of so-so, it was horizontal.

We played this game for forty-five minutes and I learned a great deal about these young Kazakhs's political opinions.

100

Khrushchev, who was then Prime Minister, came out thumbs down. Interestingly, Stalin was down. Most of the Russians I could think of were down. President Kennedy, who was then our President, came out horizontal, and most Westerners were this way or down. The only two people who came out thumbs up quickly were Genghis Khan and Kubla Khan. Mongol nationalism was not dead.

If any Russians had been watching the game, they would have been terribly apprehensive. After fifty years of bolshevism, and after a long period of trying to instill in Kazakhs, Uzbeks, and others a sense of deep pride in the Soviet Union, one still senses a certain commitment to historical racial affinities in this part of Asia. I cite this because I think it is important to recognize that race is a factor in one's emotional and political reactions, and is so around the world.

Broad racial stereotypes have been connected with Western-Asian relations since at least the beginning of the modern era, and probably since the beginning of time. One need only recall some of the classic racial depictions and expressions that influenced peoples of both areas over long periods. On the Western side, even a great leader like Winston Churchill could talk about the Asian hordes with that kind of roll of the tongue that suggested limitless peoples pouring over the steppes. In more recent times we still hear of the yellow peril. The cruel, treacherous Oriental stereotype has influenced successive generations. Within Asia, the big-nosed Westerner, the blue-eyed, red-haired barbarian, and white imperialism have been equally pervasive concepts, conveyed via pictures, literature, and the spoken word.

Racial attitudes involving "East-West" relations take an enormous number of forms, from the very crude to the extremely subtle, from the strongly derogatory to the highly eulogistic, from the unconscious and apolitical to the conscious, purposeful, and deeply political. For example, let us take a brief look at the complex of American "racial" attitudes toward Asia over the past century, admitting that this must be largely an impressionistic survey. I should also make it clear at the outset that I shall be using terms like "racial attitudes" in a very broad sense, applying these to any generalizations, favorable or unfavorable, that are intended to cover ethnic or racial categories.

The most pronounced American attitude toward Asians in the nineteenth century was probably a feeling of enormous difference. Translated into the vernacular, Asians were "upside down." Their manner of dress, eating customs, language, and all other aspects of their life were extraordinarily strange. Perhaps "bizarre" best captures the mood running through American thought and writing about Asia in this period. Every American circus and side-show had its "wild man of Borneo," ring-necked Burmese lady, or a Chinese mistress with bound feet. Such "oddities" were also featured in much of the popular writing and in travelogue lectures. Even the few serious works on Asia frequently emphasized the unusual.

This stress upon the bizarre was not overtly coupled with hostility or disdain. Rather, it reflected a natural fascination with the unusual that can spawn a type of friendliness, albeit a rather superficial type based upon curiosity, difference, and the value of being rare rather than upon compatibility. It should be emphasized, however, that the most intense American emotions of the nineteenth century in the political sphere, if one excepts the Negro issue, pertained to ethnic, not racial divisions and centrally involved the home front and Europe. Our emotional energies were largely occupied with the problem of assimilating significant numbers of Irish, Italian, Slavic, and Anglo-Saxon immigrants—many of whom retained strong ties with the "old world" as it was popularly called. The problem of establishing some principle of coexistence for Protestant, Catholic, and Jew was interrelated. It would be wise to remember that such ethnic and religious considerations far outweighed all other matters in shaping the emotional-political attitudes of the American scene.

There is no question that the political culture of the United States (to use an imprecise, and, at this juncture, possibly dangerous term) was strongly influenced by the great migrations in a fashion that bears upon our later attitudes toward Asia and the Asians. On the one hand, ethnic prejudices ran deep, reflecting the intense competition and significant cultural differences that characterized the situation. These prejudices, moreover, were often intensified by being held in the burgeoning ghettos of the large cities, and by the fact that the immigration to the United States came in waves, with complex relations developing between "early" and "late" arrivals. On the other hand, however, American ideology rested upon the egalitarian myth, and that myth was fortified in some measure at least by the extraordinary economic growth and social mobility of this era.

It was natural, therefore, to make assimilation a primary requisite, a supreme test. An egalitarian society permits only a single standard, in the broadest cultural sense. It does not readily tolerate hierarchy—nor difference, except within the bounds prescribed. Paradoxically, an egalitarian society always contains a strong quotient of both radicalism and conformity—a radical approach to status and mobility, but an insistence upon conformity to popularly derived values and goals. Twentieth-century America thus inherited a very complex culture containing within it significant elements of prejudice and at least equally significant drives toward acceptance based upon assimilation. Indeed, most ethnic groups in the United States were en route to assimilation as the new century began, and at the mid-century point, this was also true of Americans of Asian and African backgrounds. The implications of this process for American attitudes toward Asians will be further developed.

Meanwhile, let us consider one additional element in the initial response of Americans to the Far East. If Asia was considered bizarre in the nineteenth century, it was also considered a region having certain high cultures. Naturally, this aspect of Asia was most emphasized by the more educated Americans who had contact with the area—our diplomats, educators, and some missionaries and merchants. The focus, moreover, was primarily upon China in this respect, at least initially. Few American museums and cultural centers, however, failed to pay some homage to Asia by the close of the nineteenth century.

The cultural impact of traditional China, indeed, was one factor in shaping the first American views of the Chinese people, and in causing China to be regarded differently than other Asian societies. The process of differentiation on the part of Americans with respect to Asian races and cultures has been at least as important as the vaguer, more diffuse, attitudes encompassing the entire area. This process of differentiation, let it be emphasized, has not necessarily produced more enlightenment or greater accuracy; nor has it always reduced crudities. Nevertheless, the changing stereotypes in vogue in the United States with respect to varying Asian peoples—on an individual basis—have been far more significant politically than generalized views concerning the region as a whole. In this sense, at least, cultural rather than racial determinants have been considered the key variable.

Throughout most of the nineteenth century, China and the Chinese were favorably depicted—on balance—in the United States. China was regarded as a major civilization, far advanced when the West was still primitive, and still possessing a vital culture. Its territorial size and population, moreover, were seen as indications that China would play a major role in the modern world. Moreover, while Chinese attitudes toward Westerners were often criticized, the official American position at least was frequently one of seeking to differentiate Americans from Europeans with respect both to policies and attitudes, and accepting Chinese decisions. This was a policy, of course, in line with our power and the role which we were prepared to play in Asia. In some measure, at least, it was also a policy that accepted China on its own terms.

The initial American attitude toward Japan was less favorable. Numerous stories about Japanese cruelty to shipwrecked seamen preceded the Perry Expedition, and in general, the image of Japan was one of a citadel of antiforeignism. The early years after the "opening" of Japan did not dispel these feelings. On the contrary, terms like "crafty," "treacherous," "narrow," and "backward" were used to characterize the Japanese, particularly those of the samurai class who were so bitterly resisting Western intrusion.

By the close of the nineteenth century, however, the stereotypes applied to China and Japan were in the process of being reversed. At this point, Americans were prepared to view Japan as a dynamic, modern-oriented nation characterized by energy, organization, and an increasing commitment to Western-style political and economic institutions. Meanwhile, China was increasingly seen as a backward, indolent society, lacking the vigor and resourcefulness to modernize, filled with depravity, cruelty, and misery. Except for a brief interlude at the time of the Revolution of 1911, this stereotype concerning China continued to dominate the American mind down to the decade of the 1930s, when the Japanese thrust toward militarism and the new role of China caused another reversion of stereotypes.

A close examination of these stereotypes suggests that assimilation was a prominent measure of acceptability abroad as well as at home. This is not to say that broader racial themes played no role. Certainly, the "yellow peril" thesis could always be used with effect upon some circles in this country, especially since it could be coupled with domestic issues, notably the issue of the Asian workers on the West Coast. This latter issue, however, included both economic and cultural considerations. Asians were a competitive threat, especially to lower economic classes of Western background. Moreover, in this period, both Chinese and Japanese immigrants were stubbornly resisting assimilation—as they were later to do in Southeast Asia. When these groups ceased to be an economic threat and began to seek assimilation, developments that started to unfold on a large scale after World War II, widespread acceptance followed.

To apply the measurement of assimilation abroad, however, was certain to be far more complex and frustrating for Americans. Up to World War II, at least, no Asian society had been able to operate the Western democratic model successfully. In the period after 1945, some successes, together with a number of failures, could be claimed. Slowly and painfully, however, circumstances forced Americans to abandon or at least modify "assimilation" as a basis for acceptance. A new criterion, that of "modernization," helped to ease the transition, since it contained many American values. While "modernization" can be and often is, applied in an ethnocentric fashion, it can also open the door to flexibility, and the door has been increasingly used by American policy-makers and educated Americans in general in recent years.

Before any further analysis of the evolution of American attitudes and policies, however, let us turn to the Asian side of the picture. Here, class and cultural distinctions are of crucial importance. No general statement covering *Asian* attitudes toward race and culture has any merit. Complex historical and geopolitical circumstances, for example, played a major role in causing marked differences in the responses of the Chinese, Japanese, and Korean elites toward the West.

Admittedly, responses to the West and attitudes toward the Westerner are different matters, and it is quite possible that behavior patterns will be closer with respect to the latter rather than to the former issue. On this question we shall comment shortly.

Westernism, in any case, evoked very different responses even within Northeast Asia alone. Traditional China, like the modern United States, demanded assimilation as the price of acceptance. The Chinese elite, indeed, divided the world into the civilized (those who accepted Sinic culture) and the barbarian. As we have noted earlier, at its roots, this is a cultural, not a racial doctrine. In practice, however, it can have strong racial overtones, because some "barbarians" can never hope (or wish) to be "civilized."

Without question, China's response to the West was greatly affected by the strong sense of cultural superiority possessed by the Chinese sociopolitical elite, and the condescending attitude which this elite generally harbored toward all manner of barbarians on the peripheries of the empire. The Westerner was seen initially as one species of barbarian, and no particular distinction was made between Americans and Europeans, despite American efforts. Moreover, the unwillingness of Chinese officials to treat Western governments as equals—indeed, the complete absence of any principles of equality and sovereignty in Chinese experience—tended to place a premium upon a Western display of force.

Force or the threat of force produced concessions and "agreements" impossible to achieve through peaceful means, given the nature of the Chinese stance. Early in the nineteenth century, a widening division within the West had already developed between those who believed that the only way to obtain "justice" and "equity" was to deal with the Asian firmly, resorting to force if necessary and never displaying any weakness, and those who urged a greater accommodation to the Asian point of view, with efforts being made to display generosity and forbearance.

It was probably inevitable that Western policies were mainly of the hardline variety. The rigidity of the Asian elitist approach was too great and the disparity of Asian-Western power too substantial to produce any other ultimate result. To have upheld the Asian traditional approach in any major degree, moreover, would have been in contradiction to the whole pattern of development in the "advanced" world. In a few decades, indeed, these same issues were to become intra-Asian as much as Western-Asian in character.

Nevertheless, cultural and racial images were implanted or furthered in the Asian mind, particularly in the elitist mind, as a result of Western imperialism. Today, those images, exaggerated, distorted, concocted, or accurate, make up a large part of the Asian political myth. That myth often, although not always, leans heavily upon Asian defensiveness and Western aggressiveness, Asian virtue and Western inequity. It provides one basis for Asian nationalism in this form, and also for the *mea culpa* type of Westernism that has interacted forcefully with that nationalism.

The combination of extensive ethnocentrism, strong feelings of superiority, and repeated defeats at the hands of more modern societies certainly produced in a significant portion of the Chinese elite an intense consciousness of their status and role versus that of other societies and elites. As is well known, when isolation and exclusivism failed as policies, the Chinese belatedly and reluctantly accepted Western technology as a weapon with which to strike back at the West, first separating that technology rigorously from values, institutions, and culture—which were to remain ineradicably Chinese. Only after the Revolution of 1911 did any sizeable number of the Chinese sociopolitical elite begin the quest for some basic synthesis between their own culture and "foreignism" in its variant forms. Only at this point did a receptivity to Western-ism, often via its Japanese adaptation, emerge as a meaningful intellectual policy stream.

Unfortunately, the "modern" Chinese elite had an extremely limited time in which to adjust to the various waves of West-ern thought and systems. The mere forty years between 1910 and 1950 witnessed the initial introduction of "liberalism" followed within only a few years by the emergence of Marxism-Leninism; the creation and failure of numerous constitutions; the increasing interest in mobilization politics, parallel to the fascist and communist movements of Europe; and recurrent wars, civil and international.

It is important to realize that traditionalism and the quest for modernity were fused into one lifetime, one generation insofar as China has been concerned. It is not surprising, there-fore, that elements of the total rejection of Westernism, of the Westerner as barbarian, of violent xenophobia have re-mained strongly imbedded in the modernization process itself. And this was the more logical because selected aspects of Western action *and* Western thought could be used to buttress such sentiments. It is fascinating, for example, to read the essays of Chinese college students studying in Japan during the first decade of this century. They had just discovered Darwin and Spencer. The survival of the fittest was much on their minds, and repeatedly, they saw the struggle as being between the yellow and white races—with the brown and black peoples being consigned to inferiority.

Racial as well as cultural feelings run deeply through the "modernizing" youth of China in this and subsequent periods. Most certainly they also exist among the old (and young) Bolsheviks who govern China today, although such sentiments are incompatible with the Marxist creed. The communists, like the Boxers, accused Western missionaries of experimenting with babies before they accused Western (American) soldiers of practicing genocide. Like the Boxers also, they have sought to exorcise Western culture in recent years. At the same time, both overtly and in a huge variety of subtle ways, they have focused attacks upon *white* imperialism and *white* revisionism, while seeking to identify themselves with the *colored* peoples of the world. The caricatures of Americans and other white "imperialists" are replete with the symbolism of the past: the big noses, the blue eyes, and other manifestations of the barbarian.

It is true, of course, that all of this is accompanied by the most intense denials of racism, the grateful acknowledgment of the support of *all* "progressives," white as well as yellow, black, and brown, and the constant affirmation that the quarrel is with "the reactionary American clique (Khrushchevites) in power," not with "the American (Soviet) people." There is no need to regard these lines as completely bogus. The old penchant for assimilation is still present, translated into a new vernacular. If a barbarian can absorb Maoist culture, he too can become Chinese. The xenophobic quality also continues high, however, and this quality can easily take on racial manifestations as it did in the past—for natural as well as for political reasons.

It is one of the interesting paradoxes that the Chinese elite has shown itself capable of interacting with the *assimilado* on an extraordinarily high level of urbanity, camaraderie, and intensity—while retaining at the same time a capacity for complete exclusiveness, whether at the individual, group, or societal level.

To make these points, however, is to present at best only a partial picture. By 1950, a considerable proportion of the Chinese sociopolitical elite had been deeply penetrated by "Westernism," and that penetration was steadily expanding. Now a few of the modern generation were truly bicultural, having been educated in foreign schools, at home or abroad, having made commitments, occupational, political, and social, that brought them into wide-ranging contacts with the West, or with Japan. Some of these individuals had themselves become assimilated into the West. Most found it possible to live in two worlds, although the problem of fusion between these worlds went largely unsolved. Social development, in the final analysis, had not yet begun to underwrite elitist preparations, thereby engendering a continuing sense of difference, cultural or environmental, but at some point also intensely personal.

The trend nevertheless was in the direction of closing the gap at elitist levels and communist victory did not seem likely at first to halt that trend, merely to redirect it. Were not Marxist-Leninists truly cosmopolitan? Had any political group within China a stronger affinity to a foreign elite than did the Chinese communists to their foreign comrades? Was not the commitment to modernity now an all-encompassing one, necessitating the widest possible network of contacts and interests?

No one could foresee that a combination of circumstances, including a series of spectacular failures, would cause the communist leaders to revert toward exclusiveness, xenophobia, and the attitudes of intense cultural superiority and rigidity reminiscent of the past. One substantial difference, however, now exists, suggesting that present trends will be reversed at some point. Not only are the pronouncements and actions of the current elite filled with contradictions, paradoxes, and ambiguities, but also the elite itself is seriously divided. More impersonally, the very thrust toward modernization upon which path China has now been irrevocably placed must cause the forces of antiforeignism and isolation to be challenged at some stage. Thus, the far more critical issue is the degree to which the Chinese cosmopolitanism and global interaction of the future will take aggressive, ultranationalist, and racist forms.

Our attention has been directed largely toward the Chinese

elite because it is its attitudes and policies that determine policies, now and for the foreseeable future. But what of the common man? At the outset, it is crucially important to appreciate the difference between the type of xenophobia derived from peasant conservatism—fear and suspicion of the strange and unknown—and the more politicized (and probably more complex) cultural-racial attitudes of the elite. The peasant can be caused to respond at either end of the spectrum: he can be roused under certain conditions to acts of violence directly or indirectly mounted on racial-cultural bases; he can also respond to the foreigner with generosity, friendship, and incredible loyalty.

Indeed, the intensity of personal relations between Asian parishioner and foreign missionary, Asian student and foreign teacher, Asian retainer and foreign employer, and Asian soldier and foreign officer has rarely been equalled in elitist relations between "equals." The political consequences of this fact, however, must be considered very limited. In the first place, in the case of a nation like China, far less than 1 percent of the total population ever had any personal contact with foreigners. The important factor, moreover, is the character and direction of the authority emanating from an indigenous source, be it village headman, district military commander, or national leader. In the Korean War, for example, rank-and-file troops who had recently been a part of the Kuomintang army fought well under communist leadership but defected as prisoners.

This is not to assert that *any* indigenous leadership can command the loyalties of the grass roots citizenry and fashion their political attitudes. In most situations, indeed, it is less the political indoctrination and more the power to command that shapes the role of the masses. The very substantial friendship for Americans as individuals and the relatively favorable image of the United States present among the people of the Soviet Union and East Europe is not the result of official indoctrination, but largely in spite of it. While the situation in China is substantially different, there is no reason to doubt that in the improbable event of a communist overthrow and a Kuomintang return to the mainland, considerable public support for the United States could be quickly developed, combined with even greater neutrality. Then, small children would run after white men not inquiring as to whether they were "Russian friends" (or more recently, "Albanian friends"), but whether they were Americans.

Neutrality or indifference, however, would be the larger force, if true sentiment could somehow be revealed. It is very easy to overemphasize the political quotient in most men. Contrary to Aristotle, man is not a political animal most of the time unless he is forced by a regime to be so. The usual problem of mobilization politics, indeed, is to sustain the political tempo initially set, avoiding the rapid development of boredom, weariness, and ultimate hostility.

Probably the common man of Communist China today does have a higher quotient of antiforeignism and latent or overt racial feelings directed against the white man than most of his counterparts in Asia. His cultural heritage, his isolation from most external currents except through the media of his government, the intense nationalism currently being cultivated, and his present stage of economic development would be conducive to that end.

In some degree, the cultural heritage of all Asian societies deeply influenced by China is similar. Thus, Japan, Korea, and North Vietnam share some of the characteristics outlined in connection with China: traditions of exclusiveness, xenophobia, an intensive sense of cultural achievement, and a substantial degree of ethnocentrism. If these factors are still present, however, varying evolutionary patterns have recently produced significant differences among these societies.

Let us begin with Japan. Fortunately, in this case, we have

some hard data, at least with respect to the average Japanese citizen. Innumerable polls testing attitudes toward foreign nations and foreigners have been taken in Japan over the past twenty-two years. They reveal three broad tendencies of considerable interest. First, Japanese in general respect the West and Westerners more than they respect Asia and the Asians. Consistently, the top scorers on such questions as "Which nation do you respect most?" or "Which country do you like most?" have been the United States and Switzerland. Moreover, Americans as individuals have tended over the years to hold a top position when similar questions are asked with respect to persons rather than nations.

Second, policy rather than race or cultural affinity appears to have been increasingly a prime factor in determining political "likes" and "dislikes." For example, throughout the occupation era and beyond, the Soviet Union consistently polled the lowest scores while the United States was polling the highest. The reason was not difficult to discern. Soviet policy toward Japan was characterized by unmitigated harshness, and the prisoner-of-war issue in particular incensed most Japanese citizens. Recently, however, an increasing number of Japanese have registered their antagonism toward Communist China. In a recent poll, one-fourth of the respondents listed China as the nation most disliked, a very sharp rise from a previous poll. The combined impact of the cultural revolution and Chinese nuclear armament has clearly produced this result. It might also be noted that the popularity of the United States has suffered somewhat from the Vietnam war (Japanese mass media have presented an almost uniformly unfavorable picture, and in very concentrated form), although the drop has not been of major proportions.

Finally, a further testing of attitudes, particularly respecting Americans, indicates a highly refined and essentially rational judgment of strengths and weaknesses. Some years ago, at the close of the occupation, respondents were asked to list the good and bad points of Americans. The three top "good points" were: generosity, a willingness to share things with others; openness and friendliness of personality; and energy, efficiency, and a capacity for hard, purposeful work. The three leading "bad points" were racial prejudice, boisterousness and ill-manners, and wastefulness. It is also to be noted that most polls have indicated that the Japanese believe that *they* respect and admire Americans more than Americans respect and admire them, although polls taken among Americans do not reveal this to be the case.

From the standpoint of human relations, the American occupation of Japan and subsequent American-Japanese relations must be acknowledged as a major success. This is true despite the fact that once again the extent of personal contact on a mass basis can easily be exaggerated. Polls indicate that no more than 10 percent of the Japanese people ever had personal contact with an American, despite the lengthy, massive presence of American forces. Nevertheless, the image was generally favorable. Why? Undoubtedly, this is an enormously complex matter, but one central factor needs to be appreciated: in policy terms, the United States was prepared to interact effectively with the urgent needs of the Japanese people; and those people, having been acculturated to the modernization process, were able to appreciate the significance of American political behavior, having a number of the same broad goals. In sum, the particular stage of development characterizing a society and its people is certain to have a major impact upon those people's perception of themselves, their attitudes toward foreigners, and their sense of identification with, or separation from, other cultures.

In the case of Japan, all indications point to a set of responses not uncharacteristic of an "advanced" society. Racial prejudice is certainly not absent from the Japanese scene, but in its crudest, most overt forms, it is directed against the

Koreans, who are regarded as "dirty, shiftless, unruly, and lacking in culture." That most Koreans in Japan came from the lowest economic class and were brought in during wartime as unskilled laborers contributes to this image, of course. Naturally, it is not uniformly held, and over time it will change. Nevertheless, it is revealing of several important facts. Whereas, for Japan, the Westerner was the barbarian in the mid-nineteenth century, and the Korean, a part of the civilized world, that picture was reversed in the course of the next century, reflective of Japan's own changing culture. Second, similar attitudes, more moderate and subdued, can be detected in the Japanese attitude toward the "underdeveloped world" in general. Japanese prejudices, in sum, whether at the mass or elitist level, are essentially those of an advanced, industrial society.

Again, this is not to suggest that all consciousness of race and color has disappeared. This is emphatically not the case. Like most Asians, Japanese generally accord lightness of skin color a much higher value than darkness. Intermarriage, however, between a Caucasian and a Japanese is not generally acceptable, and the prejudice against mixed-blood children, whether conceived in or out of wedlock, has been pronounced. At elitist levels, moreover, attitudes respecting the Westerner, and particularly the American, are further complicated by a range of political and psychological considerations.

The Japanese intellectuals, for example, have in a number of cases developed a rather strong love/hate relationship involving respect, jealousy, intimacy, frustration, insecurity, and a host of other emotions. It is fashionable in Japanese intellectual circles to be anti-American in policy terms, often in a most irresponsible manner. Pressed, however, the Japanese intellectual will reveal that he can be anti-American more comfortably because he does not anticipate any personal repercussions, does not expect such attitudes necessarily to interfere with his ties with

America, and also regards his "understanding" of America as sufficient to permit this type of behavior. Attitudes toward the Soviet Union, Communist China, and such states as India, on the other hand, are almost always extremely cautious, guarded, and forbearing. Here, the intellectual is more ill at ease, more uncertain, and hence more circumspect. None of this should be taken, however, as indicative of the inner values the intellectual possesses, or political choices he would make if forced to do so.

A younger generation of Japanese intellectuals is now emerging. They are beginning to cast off the outmoded Marxist framework which hobbled many older intellectuals. This new avant-garde is pragmatic, realistic, and oriented toward science and social science in its more modern forms. Once again, this transition is a product of a given stage of development. In the course of the next decade, it is likely to alter still more the general manner in which Japanese look at themselves and at others.

Already, the Japanese business, professional, and conservative political elites have moved far in the direction of a pragmatic, modernist, self-confident approach to political and social problems. The traditional inferiority complex which marked Japan as a society apart from China has been reduced substantially among the groups mentioned above. The most meaningful question to be asked, indeed, might be whether a psychology more akin to "Gaullism" will develop within such groups. It should be noted, incidentally, that the intensely hierarchical character of the Japanese social system has not made easy either the conceptualization or the practice of relationships marked by equality. This is one reason why the idea of an alliance of equals is so difficult for the Japanese to perceive, and why also the type of intimacy in personal relations with foreigners characteristic of precommunist American-Chinese relations has been far more rare. In sum, in the case of Japan, a number of basic cultural attributes worked against an acceptance of the American, whereas developmental patterns worked powerfully for it; in the case of China, almost the reverse has come to be true.

Korea is an arresting case, partly because one can study a people remarkably homogeneous in their cultural evolution up to 1945 despite a stormy history, now dramatically split as a result of World War II. In many respects, Korean society traditionally represented the most conservative society within the Confucian orbit, and in the classic sense, the most "anti-foreign." The term "hermit Kingdom," often applied by early observers, symbolized this aspect of Korean attitudes. Certain rational considerations were also involved. The location of Korea and its relatively small size combined to make Koreans exceedingly wary of complicating, external relations.

Nevertheless, rationality also contributed to an opposite result. A significant portion of the Korean sociopolitical elite has been forced for nearly a century to align itself with some major foreign power or powers for self-protection. And from the end of the nineteenth century, one portion of that elite saw the United States as a logical protector because it was big, growing in power, far away, and with minimal needs for self-aggrandizement in the northeast Asian area. The affinity between the Korean elite and the United States was abetted by certain personal ties, overwhelmingly religious. For the modern Korean, Christianity became a method of expressing political as well as religious sentiments—a source of nationalist identification against Chinese and Japanese threats.

Via Christianity and enforced exile, a sizeable proportion of the modern Korean elite has broken with the isolationist, Confucianist, Sinocentric past, although the profound conservatism of the rural areas, at least in the South, still tends to exist. The rural-urban gap in South Korea is very pronounced, although almost everywhere in Asia it has been of vital significance. This gap, moreover, closely approximates the elite-mass gap. The elite, partaking of the same cultural tradition as the masses, have sharpened, shaped, and altered their prejudices and attitudes toward other races and nations in accordance with both political and personal considerations. Nationalism in Asia is still essentially an elitist, urban phenomenon. In Korea, as a result of the colonial experience, it quite naturally took anti-Japanese forms, and hence, prejudice against the Japanese in elitist nationalist circles ran higher than against any other nationality or state. The Korean peasant, however, was not and essentially is not anti-Japanese. A significant portion of the Korean elite itself accepted assimilation into the Japanese empire over time, it should be stated, but for the peasant, that was almost uniformly true.

Thus, South Korea represents a society in which the political elite has established close relations with the West, particularly the United States, for very rational reasons, at present, buttressing its position via new ties with Japan. Gradually, these political relations have become cultural ones, generally at a pace much less rapid than in the case of Japan because of the slower progress of socioeconomic evolution. Since the Korean hinterland, for example, still lies largely outside the perimeters of "the new culture," its attitudes are still strongly the traditional ones.

On the other hand, among the younger Korean intellectuals, one can detect the emergence of some of the same love/hate attitudes toward the United States as have long been characteristic of Japanese intellectual positions. At the same time, however, as a result of their close relationship with current American scholarship, a number of younger Korean intellectuals now have a technical competence in the social sciences more advanced than their Japanese counterparts. South Korea represents an interesting laboratory, therefore, in which to study the interaction between conflicting "emotional" and "rational" elements, sometimes operative within the same individual.

Despite the reasonably close relations that have existed between a certain portion of the Korean elite and Americans, one political transition of significance has taken place in Korea since 1961. An older generation of political leaders dominated by strongly Westernized types (many of them long-time exiles in the West) has been succeeded by a younger, more Asian set of leaders, in this case, military. The new leadership is less acculturated to the West, and less close to Westerners in personal terms, but not necessarily "anti-Western." This major transition, moreover, is underway in almost all parts of ex-colonial Asia, with potentially far-reaching repercussions in the decades that lie immediately ahead.

To release elites from the psychological burdens of colonialism could not be accomplished in less than one, possibly two, generations. Characteristic of Nehru, Sukarno, and leaders of similar backgrounds were a series of giant paradoxes and conflicts: an intense emotional commitment to many aspects of Western culture, including Western political values and institutions, yet a deep resentment of Western policies and behavioral patterns, and a rising frustration as the result of failures to adapt Westernism successfully to indigenous conditions; a strong nationalism and love of one's people in the abstract but a profound separation from the "common man" in attitudes, values, and pattern of life—and a very mixed attitude toward the culture, with sentiments of contempt, disgust, and anger competing with those of love, admiration, and acceptance; and finally, a feeling of being compartmentalized—of living simultaneously a number of different lives, and hence, searching endlessly for a personal as well as a national identity.

Operating under these conditions, the attitude of Asian elites in ex-colonial situations toward other cultures and races, and particularly toward America and Americans, necessarily has been extraordinarily complex. For example, some of Nehru's anti-Americanism derived from his Cambridge education, not from India. Indeed, the Sorbonne, Oxford, Cambridge, and a host of other European centers of higher education have contributed much to the cultural attitudes and prejudices of the first-generation, postcolonial leadership in Asia and Africa. Beyond that, however, the tangled nature of their own lives and their relation with their own countrymen make inevitable a highly complex set of attitudes with respect to other peoples.

This first-generation elite tended to hold cosmopolitanism as a faith while harboring deep prejudices of a cultural and racial character as a result of their own experiences, real and fancied, and the enormous psychological burdens of colonialism. If they turned to Marxism, cultural and racial prejudices could be cloaked in class terms, but in most cases they were not altered basically. At present, however, a new, younger generation is emerging, less scarred by the past, more attuned to their own people, less cosmopolitan and more indigenous, and generally less ideological and more pragmatic, problem-oriented, and administrative in character. It is possible that this generation will be less prone to cultural and racial generalizations, just as they are likely to be less prone to a cosmic political faith.

Certainly, the thrust of the current political elite in South Korea is in this direction. At some risk, the present leaders were even willing to normalize relations with Japan, thereby throwing down the gauntlet to the older, orthodox nationalist movement. North Korea, however, presents a strikingly different picture in most respects, one far more closely resembling trends in Communist China despite the present estrangement between these two governments. North Korea is currently in a Stalinist phase, dominated by the cult of personality, mobilization politics, and a high measure of isolation from the world.

An unprecedented volume of hate dominates the propaganda disseminated by the elite to the masses, and while this hate is ideologically and class oriented, much of it has the same cultural and racial overtones characteristic of contemporary Chinese communist propaganda.

North Korea thus presents an image of a society based upon total mobilization and near-total alienation from states and peoples not prepared for assimilation. Have communist elitist values and attitudes been successfully transmitted to the average citizen? Have the Korean communists created a new Soviet man? Has Korean nationalism of the communist variety been able to tap successfully the traditional resources of anti-foreignism, exclusivism, and isolation? We have no way of answering these questions with any degree of accuracy, but in the absence of additional data, our hypotheses would be similar to those advanced concerning China. Undoubtedly, Kim Il-sung like Mao Tse-tung (and Ho Chi Minh), has been successfully projected as a father-figure, and for vast numbers of people symbolizes authority. Communism has been personalized; it has not been institutionalized. It is probably also true that prolonged, saturation-type indoctrination has had some influence. It would not be surprising to find that the anti-American views of the average North Korean were pronounced.

Nevertheless, an effective, decisive change in top political authority would probably cause an alteration in mass attitudes rather more quickly than would be thought possible. Moreover, the basic contradictions built into the current policies and goals of the Korean communist elite promise to raise new crises of an ideological and attitudinal nature. In sum, the movement from ideology to pragmatism, from first-generation revolutionaries to second-generation administrators which can be discerned in most noncommunist societies of Asia, will ultimately affect the communist societies, although not necessarily with the same political results insofar as the external world is concerned.

It remains to apply briefly some of the theses advanced above to Southeast Asia, the last area with which we shall be concerned here. It is crucial at the outset to underline one vitally important factor with respect to this region: almost without exception, the most important racial tensions in Southeast Asia are among the peoples living there. These tensions involve three types of relations, speaking in very broad terms: first, the Chinese and Indian problems, with the Chinese problem being acute in most of the region; second, relations between the "valley" and the "hills" peoples, between the "advanced," rice-growing peoples and the "primitive" subsistence agriculture and hunting peoples, again a problem endemic to the entire area, and often of major proportions; finally, "refugee" or "enclave" problems involving different ethnic groups such as the Vietnamese in Thailand or the Cambodians in South Vietnam.

When to these racial or ethnic issues are added an additional range of conflicts that are regional or religious in nature, the problems of nation-building in Southeast Asia begin to assume their true proportions. And indeed, only the Philippines and Thailand have achieved any substantial degree of integration at this point, with even these two societies facing serious problems.

For the average Southeast Asian, even for the elite of the area, the above problems generally take precedence over other issues of a cultural or racial character, and shape attitudes toward such questions. For example, historically, one function of the Western colonial power was to protect ethnic minorities, especially "backward" ones, against more advanced, assertive elements within the society. The basic dissatisfaction of such minorities throughout the region today is attributable to the fact that no one is playing that role, least of all the indigenous governments composed of ethnic majorities.

Dissatisfaction, moreover, extends over a much broader segment of the population in many regions. *Pax Europa* has been removed, and what has been instituted in its place? The peasant is above all concerned about sufficient stability to protect his life and that of his family; he makes only minimal demands on his government, whether in the form of labor, taxes, or military service and hopes for some advances with respect to material goods, food, and education for his children. New governments have performed better on these scores in very few cases thus far, probably mainly in the field of education. There is little reason, therefore, for the peasant to regard the colonial experience in a highly negative fashion, or to have that experience bring a sharper focus to antiwhite sentiments. The peasant may well have retained his suspicion of any foreigner, but he reserves his overt hostility generally for those who trouble him with immediate problems, competition, or their mere presence. It is the Chinese, the Shan, the Naga, and the Meo against whom he reacts.

Does this situation change in the midst of foreign presence, such as in the case of Vietnam? The polls taken thus far in South Vietnam are probably not scientific enough to be judged reliable, but indications do not suggest a markedly dissimilar pattern to that which we have drawn. Ethnic minorities, particularly the hills people, actively cooperate with Americans in most cases, but act in a very reserved fashion at best toward the Vietnamese. The Vietnamese peasant in overwhelming measure is apolitical, struggling to survive under very precarious circumstances. He has not committed himself voluntarily to the National Liberation Front in significant numbers, although when his village is occupied, he obeys NLF instructions. His attitude toward the government is similar. Nor is there evidence of extensive anti-Americanism among the peasantry except under professional guidance, although fear, suspicion, and other "traditional" forms of behavior are certainly commonplace, along with gratitude, respect, and affection after good treatment. The touchstone, however, is security, and all overt attitudes are to be measured against the delivery or non-delivery of this one, vital commodity.

Anti-Americanism is certainly present, and possibly even growing among some elements of the sociopolitical elite, depending upon political views, personal treatment, and similar matters. It is not, however, a major element if recent polls can be trusted. The Vietnamese do believe that they like Americans better than Americans like them, a common reaction as we have noted earlier. The average Vietnamese also shows relatively strong dislike for, or suspicion of, both the Chinese and the hills people, for different reasons, of course. Regional differences, moreover, are pronounced, as are religious divisions. Vietnam, in short, is a microcosm of Southeast Asia, particularly of the ex-colonial sectors of that region.

What conclusions can be drawn from this complex, variegated picture of cultural and racial attitudes? Clearly, a consciousness of race is present both in the United States and throughout the Far East. On balance, however, the modernization process has operated to reduce racial stereotypes operating in pure form, whether at the domestic or the international level. That process has generally moved political behavior in the direction of the rational through an advancement of education, economic values, and social mobility. Exclusivism and isolation have been challenged. At the same time, of course, new racial tensions have developed in the form of radically uneven development, on the one hand, and more intense competition in some areas for jobs, housing, and similar matters, on the other. It is precisely out of these developments that the domestic racial tensions of "advanced" societies mount.

However, such domestic crises do not necessarily translate

themselves into the increased application of racial stereotypes in attitudes relating to international politics, or even such application directed toward racial groups within the society other than those frontally engaged. Differentiation, moreover, tends to extend even into the groups centrally involved in "modernized" societies. Thus, to *most* whites, there are "good" and "bad" Negroes, and issue- or action-orientation tends to mitigate racial generalizations, even when these are voiced or felt in considerable measure. This also applies to Negro attitudes toward whites.

In certain terms, the drive for assimilation, strongly characteristic of the United States both at home and abroad until recently, and now a hallmark of the Asian communist regimes, also modifies pure racial themes. Assimilation, at least in theory, is predicated upon the assumption that all individuals and groups are capable of such identification. There is little doubt, however, that assimilation doctrines, strongly held and pursued, can in fact abet doctrines of racial or cultural superiority. This, indeed, is one of the significant problems of Chinese communist interrelation with the world today, just as it was one prominent aspect of American, one might say Western, interaction with the nineteenth and early twentieth-century world, an aspect that lingers on in many circles.

Nevertheless, broad stereotypes pertaining to Asia such as "the yellow peril" or "the Asian hordes" have generally been replaced with much more particularized, nationally oriented generalizations. Thus, the Chinese communists, not without reason, are regarded with deep concern, whereas Americans look hopefully to Japan and the Japanese. An identity in particular with "advanced" or "democratic" societies has supplanted to a considerable extent "pure" racial concepts.

Within Asia, a not dissimilar set of circumstances applies with respect to Japan, the sole "modern" society of the region. Japan too has had a long history of deep racial consciousness, one that continues, both at elitist and mass levels. That consciousness, however, is now moderated or shaped by a host of factors—many of which involve "rational," policy- and action-oriented considerations, and substantial differentiations within and among "racial" categories. Quite clearly, moreover, political generalizations can change within the compass of a short period of time, depending upon developments in the political world. Polls, both in Japan and in the United States, challenge any thesis that racial considerations are paramount factors in either elitist or mass political attitudes.

The communist states of Asia, as we have noted, constitute a special problem, because in each of them the elite consciously emphasizes a policy containing within it a heavy component of hate, exclusivism, and isolation, protestations to the contrary notwithstanding. Since all the currently operating Asian communist states (with the partial exception of Mongolia) earlier lay within the Confucian orbit, traditional proclivities toward ethnocentrism and xenophobia can be used and abetted. Racial-cultural feelings, translated into a somewhat new political vernacular, may be on the ascendency in these societies. *At this particular stage of modernization*, therefore, they may represent exceptions to our early thesis about the relationship between modernization and racial attitudes. In the long run, however, we have argued that racially-culturally oriented views will be challenged in a modernizing communist state as in other such states, especially given the degree of ambivalence in communist theory and policies.

Racial attitudes in the "emerging" portions of non-Communist Asia are infinitely more complex, especially in those regions until recently under Western colonial control. The available evidence does not suggest intense anti-Western feelings at the mass level (or in the case of the Koreans, anti-Japanese feelings at that level). From a purely rational standpoint, as we have indicated, the common Southeast Asian was at least as well off in material terms prior to World War II as he has been since that time. His more immediate racial concerns have been domestic ones, which have been intense, and continue to constitute a major obstacle to internal political stabilization.

For the first-generation political elite of the region, the issues were considerably more complex. Certainly a love/hate relationship toward the West and the Westerner developed. This involved complex psychological problems that could never be satisfactorily solved by that generation. Now, however, a younger, postcolonial *Asia-centered* elite is emerging, less constricted by the scars of the past and at least potentially more capable of viewing issues in policy- and action-oriented terms.

At the moment, racial-ethnic attitudes in southern Asia tend to be most intense as they relate to "indigenous" peoples versus overseas Chinese and Indians; valley people versus hill people; and "northerners" versus "southerners." In these struggles, both elite and masses are perfectly willing to enlist the support of "foreigners" of a different race and culture, particularly if they have reason to believe that those "foreigners" will be relatively altruistic and self-effacing.

It remains to suggest briefly some of the implications of these hypotheses, if valid, for American foreign policy in East Asia. First, it is surely time to get rid of the *mea culpa* attitude which infests so much American liberal thinking in particular about our past and present role. It is not necessary to designate American policies as perfect or near-perfect in order to note their successes as well as their failures, discover the very substantial progress in sophistication that has been made, and define the problems in a realistic, nonsentimental fashion.

In this connection, someone ought to bury the old myth that "the white man's day in Asia is over." When it was first uttered in the heyday of Western imperialism, it no doubt had a very useful purpose. To those who subscribe to theses like that of "black power" and other forms of apartheid, it still does. But it bears scant relation to the basic needs of Asia, or its middle- and long-range problems. To put it succinctly, Asia and America have never needed each other so much, and the thesis that risk can be avoided, or better avoided, by the isolation of these two dynamic regions is sheer nonsense.

The issue is what types of interaction are possible, potentially constructive, and feasible? The first prerequisite for an Asia that can contribute to its own peace and stability and that of others is a broad, overarching political equilibrium. Without this, it is useless to talk of economic and social development, although these must be tackled simultaneously with the task of seeking a balance of power and nation-building. The United States must play a major role in the quest for political equilib- rium, because no other noncommunist nation is prepared to do so. No amount of handwringing or exhortation will change that elemental fact of political life.

This will require a fairly substantial American military presence in or near the Far East for a considerable period of time. But there are many crucial issues to be raised and settled in this respect. American bases in or near populous Asian centers, for example, are almost certain to cost a heavier and heavier political price. The temptation will be to divert atten- tion from domestic crises of a political, economic, or ethnic type to an "external" target, but one immediately available. Military technology must come to grips with this political reality, and it must do so in the proper time. The timing of such policies, indeed, is at least as important as their content. We must move now to reduce or eliminate all potential sources of blackmail, even from our friends, while not making the grave mistake of seeking a return to isolation and hence an advance to World War III.

Coupled with these concerns, we must seek to develop the concept of partnership, a relation of equals. This in most cases involves primarily our relations with Asian elites. On the one hand, we must perfect a new style of politics, one that solicits ideas, listens to suggestions, and, as the Japanese would say, adopts a "low posture." At the same time, we must work to close the responsibility gap by insisting that Asian societies, particularly those in a better position, bear an increased responsibility for economic, political, and military policies involving the area as a whole. Partnership is a two-way street, and we have not progressed along either side sufficiently at this point.

One of our great tasks at this point is to aid in the training of the second-generation elite. This elite, pragmatic, administrative, problem-oriented, can begin to act as a modernizing force, and reverse the ever-widening gap between "advanced" and "backward" states that makes both so susceptible to racial and cultural stereotypes. At present, for example, even in sophisticated policy circles, it is convenient to speak of "soft" and "hard" societies, thereby describing in short-hand the differences, let us say, between the Burmese and the Chinese. These stereotypes have some validity, but it is vitally important to help "soft" societies develop some coherence and commitment without thrusting them onto the path of totalitarianism. Here, the role of the second-generation revolutionaries is a crucial one.

If these are desirable American-Asian policies with respect to elites, what about the common man? It has been said that the United States has a common man's culture, and it ought to make the most of it—rock and roll, gadgets, movies and all. This is at least partially valid. American "culture," measured in these terms, is a powerful influence of a mixed character, no doubt. In general, moreover, the American as an individual is liked by the Asian common man. An excessive presence, however, particularly in cases where the military situation demands the temporary stationing of large numbers of American soldiers, inevitably represents a threat. In many cases, it is just as important to keep peoples aloof from each other as it is to encourage mixing. More accurately, the key to a successful policy in the long run is that policy which manages to encourage appropriate elements to engage in cultural exchange both at elitist and grass roots levels while seeking to discourage or prevent this on an indiscriminate mass basis. Some individuals and groups, sent abroad for much needed functional purposes, should be given maximum base entertainment and segregated as much as possible from the indigenous society, whereas interaction at this point between mature, balanced American intellectuals and their Asian counterparts has never been more badly needed.

Each of these policy considerations relates to one central and all-important thesis. The issues to be faced in America's Asian policy are issues of gradation and mix, not those of all or nothing. Our challenge is to build a set of incremental policies—sophisticated, intricate, and multiple. To refight the battle along such simplistic lines as "intervention" versus "isolation" is not only foolish—it is wasteful. The issues are no less important—and no less exciting intellectually—if one places them in more complex, technical, and realistic terms. Thus, in the final analysis, the challenge is to American culture. To a very considerable measure, we have moved away from an assimilationist complex in the past two decades. Can we now summon the patience to live with policies attuned to that fact without toppling backward into an isolationist stance?

# 6 Race and National Cohesion in Latin America

*Kalman H. Silvert*

I would like to address myself first to the question of community in Latin America, then to the relationship between community and race, and finally to the relations among community, race, and power. I will choose examples from diverse countries in order to illustrate the range of social occurrences in Latin America and offer several subjective estimates concerning relations among community organization, race, power, and international affairs. This task is grandiose, but I will do my best not to skip too much of prime significance.

As has so often been noted, the twenty Latin American republics present many social variations. Thus we are dealing with a problem in comparison, not alone among the republics but within each one. We must distinguish between those countries which are so internally fragmented that we cannot legitimately speak even in averages concerning them, and those republics which are rather homogeneous in their ethnic composition and social order. For example, a little country like Uruguay has a population of some 2.5 million, practically all of them of European descent. Similarly, about 96 percent of Argentina's population is of European-descent: Italians, Spanish, a few Portuguese, Germans, Yugoslavs, Russians, Poles—that is, the country has a population composition similar to that of the United States, minus black populations and with a smaller percentage of Anglo-Saxons. But then we also have a country like Brazil, with a population of 80 million, part of it European, part Oriental, part Indian, another part Negroid, and all randomly distributed, with the result that little of what is socially true of southeast Brazil is also true of northeast Brazil.

The history of man tells us that: in the beginning we were nomads, and then after a while we became seminomads. From being hunters and fishermen we turned to cultivating wild grain. Then, as we mastered grain production, we settled down into villages. Later, from an isolated village structure we moved to a feudal universalistic structure and then into the early form of the city-state and the nation-state, until finally we arrived at the present national community. If one stands this history of human community on end, it describes the entire spread which can be found in contemporary Brazil. There are nomads, seminomads, isolated village communities, feudal universalistic enclaves, and commercial cities of a mercantilistic type; in addition, there is a modern, industrial, urban Brazil. It is because of this diversity that generalization is meaningless for Brazil. A per capita income figure, for example, in a country in which money means qualitatively different things for different parts of the population, is obviously meaningless. It is like adding Cadillacs to oranges and then attempting to strike a mean.

In another category still are countries like Guatemala which, instead of being cut in as many different directions as Brazil with its numerous different shades and colors and tones intertwined in the population, is essentially a two-toned country—

partly Indian and partly what Guatemalans call *Ladino* and Mexicans call *mestizo*—that is, a mixture of European and Indian. About half the population of Guatemala lives in Indian culture, the other half in Ladino or European culture.

Argentina, Brazil, and Guatemala represent three prototypical families of social organization in Latin America. The predominantly Indian-mestizo countries can be listed very easily. They are Guatemala, Colombia outside the cities, Ecuador, Peru, Bolivia, and Paraguay. The mixed but culturally predominantly mestizo countries include Brazil, Mexico, Cuba, the Dominican Republic, Venezuela, Nicaragua, Honduras, El Salvador, and Panama. The predominantly European countries are Costa Rica, Chile, Argentina, and Uruguay. (Haiti is an exception, of course, with citizens almost exclusively of African origin.) Relationships among ethnic groups clearly will differ among these types of countries.

## A Cultural Definition of Race

It is wise to stop at this moment and begin to define what is meant by the word "race." A Guatemalan Indian is shedding his "Indianness" when he begins to speak Spanish, when he takes off his Indian costume and puts on a pair of sandals, khaki pants, and a European shirt, and when he leaves his village. That list represents the cost of his limited admission into the European community. The definition of what is to be mestizo or ladino or Guatemalan is not racial in a physical anthropological sense, but rather cultural. If a Guatemalan Indian acquires the earmarks of European culture, he can begin to cross, although the rest of the ladino community does not in that instant accept him. His partial passage does mean, however, that, other things being equal, his child will be accepted as a full member of the ladino community with whatever other characteristics, costs, and benefits may be involved in that status. The process is not that simple in Peru, and there are many variants on these mobility patterns. But, essentially, when Latin Americans say *"raza,"* they are not describing a man's skin color or the configuration of his facial bones, or his slouch, or the way he walks, or whether or not he has an epicanthic fold, they are describing his culture and not his physical characteristics.

Chile provides an example in another kind of setting. It is probable, by the measurements of some physical anthropologists, that about 40 percent of the Chilean population, which I have characterized as being European, is in physical terms mestizo. On my first trip to Chile in the summer of 1947, I was talking with a Chilean with a very dark bronze skin, sparkling deep brown eyes, jet-black hair, and very high cheek bones in a broad face. He said to me, "There aren't any Indians in this country." Dressed in a white suit which accentuated his complexion, he looked unmistakably Indian, but he was not speaking of looks. The point is obvious: "Indian-ness" is not recognized as a physical characteristic in Chile. Correlatively, skin color is not "seen" as a racial and hence caste-defining fact.

Nevertheless, in every Latin American country, color is indeed seen as a class fact. We had a maid once in Chile who was a combination of Japanese, Araucanian Indian, and European. We used to test out questionnaires on many persons, and one day when I was out of the house my wife was talking to the maid about the language of a questionnaire concerning social organizations and social structure. My wife asked her what an upper-class person looked like. The girl said, "Well, everyone knows what an upper-class person looks like—tall, blond, blue-eyed." A little bit later my wife thought to ask her, "How would you describe my husband?" Sure enough, I came out tall, blond, blue-eyed. The reason is quite obvious. The upper class in Chile was for a very long time composed predominantly of Basques, persons from northern Spain, many of whom are tall, blond, and blue-eyed. In addition, there is a pervasive cultural jealousy of the prototypical Anglo-Saxon —tall, blond, blue-eyed. What overrode my real physical characteristics was the superimposed identification of physical appearance and class position. The maid described me as a member of a class, not as an individual.

Race in Latin America—where it is a problem—is more a class matter than an ethnic one, except in the highly Indian countries. This conclusion stems even from the process of a Guatemalan Indian becoming a ladino, however. If the definition is cultural, then we are in effect saying that persons are not held in race bondage because of their nature, nor because they are thought to be of a qualitatively different species from others. Rather, they are held in class bondage as members of a lower social order within an all-embracing universe. The rank ordering of the classes is *accompanied* by color changes but is not *determined* by them.

The distinction between viewing certain groups as qualitatively different from others and as differing inside the same universe sometimes spells a distinction between life and death. The operators of German concentration camps, for example, managed to avoid empathizing with their victims. They avoided identifying with their victims by saying that the victim does not feel the same as others, by saying, in effect, that he is not human. So the people who worked in the German concentration camps could look upon the persons whom they put in the gas ovens the same way that ASPCA employees look upon the dogs that they execute. The difference between a racial categorization—qualitatively isolating groups—and a class categorization—setting aside persons inside a universe of equals—is also a way of defining the nature of community.

In Latin American countries race conflict is not of the same order as in the United States, the reason being that the basic values of the society do not read Indians out of humanity. Thus, such articles can be written as " 'Race' Relations without Conflict," one of the best-known anthropological articles on Guatemalan Indians. Thus, too, mythology can hold that in Brazil there is no racial tension. Indeed there is, but it takes the form of class tension reinforced by color visibility. The lower one goes in the social order, the darker the skin tone—a formula true in every Latin American country. Color makes mobility more difficult, but not impossible.

## Relationship between Race and Class

Keeping in mind the differences among Latin American countries, the three general families of racial situations, and the distinction between stratification by race and by class, we can now begin to explore the relationship between class divisions and national cohesion, and between race divisions and national cohesion. We need to take this second step in order to get the third one concerning the position of Latin America on the international scene as affected by intranational social organization. In classical Marxist fashion we could say that class conflict exists every place in the world where classes exist, that by definition there are classes in every reasonably developed society, and that therefore—since race correlates highly with class and since all classes are in conflict with all other classes—what we have in Latin America is class conflict that generally equals race conflict. But that statement is not empirically supportable, because class and race do not correlate directly in Latin America. There is blurring across the color lines, and comparisons of class-race relations do not hold steady across national boundaries. In Mexico the national upper class is mestizo, and leading political positions are reserved for mestizos. The same is generally true in Venezuela, but not so in Uruguay or Argentina, and it certainly is not the case in Chile or Costa Rica.

It is also not empirically valid to maintain that classes tend to have cohesive notions of what their class interest may be. We do not find with any degree of regularity that social groups which we can call classes have developed class consciousness and that income-occupation class groups act with high degrees of cohesiveness or congruence, particularly in situations of rapid social change. When I refer to social classes, then, I do not mean cohesive interest groups acting within predictable ideological constraints, but rather clusterings of persons who generally share the same power levels. Class refers to potential power and its distribution, which means it is a categorization of the latent power belonging to sets of individuals, and nothing else. For my purposes, class is a conglomerate category concerning the economic, social, and political power an individual or group can bring to bear in given situations; it is a power measure, not an ideology measure. It does not tell us what persons will do with their power, and it does not measure personality. Therefore, all I am saying is that the darker one's skin tone in Latin America, generally the less power he has. To put the matter in this way may seem simplistic, but it frees the analysis of unwanted ideological freight.

The relationship between class and total community is very complex. The primary hypothesis I should like to suggest is that every society modernizes as it tends toward a greater urban style for its population, toward impersonal work relationships or an industrial-economic life style, and toward rewarding persons for their merit instead of for the ascriptive situation in which they find themselves because of their birth and their friendship patterns. As a society becomes modern in these senses, it obviously also becomes more highly stratified. Sociologists and political scientists call these trends the development of institutional specificity and of institutional differentiation.

Most social commentators have put the accent of their research on the facts of specialization. I should like to suggest that putting the accent only on what divides societies is not good enough for the purposes of political analysis. One needs to know not only what cuts a society into pieces, but also what makes it cohere. Every developed society has found means to prevent class differences from tearing it to pieces, to paste the differentiating effects of class structures into a whole. Though many devices are used to accomplish this melding, the principal political device is the nation-state which incorporates the ideology of nationalism, an appropriate legal structure, and the value systems that make national community cohesive. In short, a system of loyalties is built into the society transcending the divisions within it.

The system of loyalties in any developed society creating supraclass identifications obviously has to be buttressed with more than a mere political component. It has to be supported with enough access to economic benefits to satisfy persons' wants in ways that will permit them to continue their identification with more favored groups. A lower-class person in the United States, for example, can usually buy himself a used automobile. An upper-class person, if he wants to, can buy a Rolls Royce. But they are both automobiles. In other countries persons at the bottom often cannot buy bicycles. The economic situation does not permit even the universe of the wheel to be shared generally across the social board.

In political terms the question concerns universal participation in deciding on the basic posture or stance of the government of that state for a given time. In short, are citizens equal before the law for the purposes of voting? Another way in which supraclass identity is certified is in the case of conflict and the resolution of conflict. Are litigants truly equal before the laws and before the courts which enforce the law, no matter the state of their pocketbooks, the accent they bring into court, and their skin color?

One could continue to multiply these examples of the institutional devices which every national society forges in order to persuade its population that a general social interest is sometimes worth pursuing over a specific class interest. In the case of the Latin American countries, by and large race does not exclude people from human community, but it does tend to group racial clusters in such a way that the lower orders are not part of the national continuum. The ethnically disfavored remains a human being, but one without access to the national institutions.

## Two Latin American Case Studies

We often unthinkingly ask what Guatemalans "think" about this or that. To answer, however, we would have to stop to define "Guatemalans." On the basis of the census of 1953 (which I choose because the numbers are easy to use, but the same percentages would hold for 1970, so the conclusions are the same) there were about 3 million persons living in Guatemala. Of that number, 53 percent were Indians; by definition they lived in Indian villages, wore Indian costume, had their own local government, religious organizations, and language. Thus, over half of the population thought of Guatemala as a city, but not as a state or nation. That leaves 1.5 million possible candidates for being cultural national Guatemalans. Of these persons (and now we are dealing only with ladinos) at least 50 percent are illiterate; the total illiteracy rate for the country is 87 percent. Having taken out all the Indians, we are left with about half the ladinos as being illiterate. We are including only those illiterates who are of school age, of course. Of the 750,000 remaining, about 40 percent are under fourteen years of age. Defining potential national Guatemalans in terms of awareness and possible political activity as being anybody who is literate, European, and over fourteen, we have a maximum of 400,000. Of that number we should expect that half are women, that others are superannuated, some are sick, and others virtually inaccessible in the countryside. It is probable, therefore, that of the 3 million total population a maximum of 250,000 can be counted as functioning individuals in the Guatemalan national political process. From this 250,000 is drawn the entire officer corps of the army, all of the teachers, professors, high school and university students, the entire civil service, all industrial managers, physicians, lawyers, pharmacists, nurses, etc. This tiny recruitment base results when a country does not have national community as its organizing political matrix.

Let us now posit another situation: a country which also has a complex ethnic background, this time composed of Europeans of many different origins, Negroes, a small admixture of Indians, and some other neighboring peoples who have drifted in. It is a typical country in that skin tone darkens down the status scale. It is somewhat atypical for Latin America, however, in that it darkens toward Negroid characteristics. Let us give this country a population of about 7.5 million. Instead of, as in Guatemala, putting only 300,000 in the capital city (10 percent) and 27,000 in the next largest city, Quezaltenango, this country has close to 2 million in the capital city, about 25 percent of the population. Let us put another 15 percent in the second largest city and let us say that about 55 percent of the total population is urban, and that furthermore nobody lives in isolated villages. Instead of Indians who go out to work their little farms and come back at night or hire themselves out to pick coffee, as in Guatemala, in this case there has been a major shift in the landholding patterns, and persons work as ranch hands earning salaries on the farm. These farms are

commercial undertakings, and much of the product is agro-
industrialized and sold abroad. We are dealing with rural factories whose employees are wage earners, mobile, and not
tied to the soil as peons, like the Guatemalan Indians. Let us
presume that everyone in this country talks Spanish, and that
its literacy rate is about 50 percent. The capital city is in the
northwestern region, and the second largest city in the south-
eastern part, and they are joined by a double-track rail line.
Other lines go east and west, there are many good ports, and
the telegraph system has been in service for over sixty years.
The entire country is electrified, and there are a score of radio
stations in the capital city and a large university supported
with U.S. know-how and capital. The country also has one
of the highest automobile accident rates in the world.

Finally, let us give this state a corrupt military government—
dictatorial, authoritarian, irrational, and increasingly desperate
in a traditional kind of way. It is not Hitler or Mussolini who
runs this little country, but a kind of traditional Latin American
authoritarian. He wants things to be quiet, to sell what he
has to sell, to steal what he wants to steal, and he wants to
be on good terms with his more powerful neighbors. He would
prefer to buy off his opposition than to kill it off. So in the
beginning of dissidence there is little death, but as opposition
begins to mount the bloodshed becomes greater.

Now let us put you in Washington on a policy-planning staff.
Both countries have governments considered inimical to the
United States. Your orders are to get rid of them! Do you have
to be a genius to know that to topple a government supported
at maximum by only 250,000 out of a 3 million population
probably is not a very difficult task? If, however, the second
country mentioned manages to create a national consensus after
the traditional authoritarianism is deposed, what then? Even
if only a third of the adult population is willing to die in de-

fense of the *patria*, the rules of the revolutionary game undergo profound change.

To this point we have hastily distinguished between a race and a class approach and have begun to show the range of occurrences in Latin America. It is necessary now to set up the conditions under which class structure serves either to reinforce the generation of power or else to maintain a country as weak and powerless.

## Failure to Develop a National Community

National community, one which truly laces varying social groups into an overarching consensual system, is the strongest and toughest form of human organization so far known. It is that form of organization which permits a platoon of soldiers to continue fighting even when the sergeant is killed. It is that kind of social cohesion that permits leaders to send soldiers out hundreds of miles away from their own front lines and trust them to retain identity and loyalty. It is also that form of organization that can permit institutional structures to change without breaking the entire system into pieces. Indeed, self-sustaining change is the critical element of open, total community organization: it prevents narrow class or sectarian interest from breaking a society down. These statements are open to serious challenge, and indeed they should not be accepted without additional conceptual refinement.

National community has the potential of creating more human diversity than any other kind of social order, assuming that it is libertarian national community of which we speak. The more primitive the social organization, the more alike each individual is to every other individual in that structure. The more advanced a society, the more individual differentiation can have its play, for society provides areas of flexibility inside an overarching synthetic construction. The efficiency of modern national organization depends on such flexibility, for it is thus able to contain a broad spread of variety in order to enjoy the greatest efficiency from the expression of the particular gifts of each individual.

In Latin America the creation of national community would in itself indicate, as for any other part of the world, the social basis of modern political organization. Latin American countries, however, would have less difficulty arriving at this stage than many other countries with racial problems because, to repeat, they largely define race as class. But most Latin American countries fall prey to their own class exclusionisms, victims of their own inability to develop a truly overriding national organization. A vicious circle is in operation, of course, for it is from weakness that strength must grow. A national government can put letters into the mail—on which it does not even put stamps—and send them out to young men saying, "Greetings, come and put yourself in a position possibly to be killed in the defense of your country." In a nation-state, mobilization is a socially enforced activity. A nonnation-state must in effect send out press gangs, and even then can never be sure of loyalty. The difference between the way the Elizabethans recruited a navy and the way we do so today describes a fundamental difference in human organization.

No Latin American country, with one exception, is in a position to recruit a citizens' army. Every one of them has armies which are either old-fashioned or mercenary and cannot be trusted in combat. The Paraguayan army of the last century reflected great community cohesion, but by and large, today's Latin American armies are employed for internal policing purposes and their use for any truly international military purpose is a smile-provoking thought. The national cohesion required to build into individuals the willingness to die in defense of the total society is lacking in countries where class interest prevails above national interest. (I am using military examples, of course, only as an example of the limits of social cohesion and loyalty.)

If this be the case in the international political sphere, the example of the weak army can be generalized to the conclusion that Latin American countries are by and large not very strong in the defense of any other of their interests—whether those interests be economic, linguistic, cultural, or political. One of the great complaints of Latin American intellectuals is that they are constantly being overrun by foreign cultural influences. Latin American political theorists are now busily engaged in developing a "theory of dependency" to explain their situation. Helio Jaguaribe, a Brazilian political scientist, is in the forefront of this movement.

Latin states are fragile structures, which of course is the reason that so many governments fall even in economically advanced states. For example, Argentina has a standard of living that is one of the fifteen highest in the world. In 1930 there were more automobiles per capita in Argentina than in either Great Britain or Sweden; Argentines consume more animal protein per capita than any other country in the world, even today. Yet highly urbanized Argentina has suffered numerous political revolutions: one in 1930, another one in 1931, then intermittent attempts until 1943, then a significant one in 1943, then the rise of Perón and his taking office in 1946, then Perón overthrown by revolution in 1955, then a short military interregnum and another revolution in 1955, then a legal election in 1957 with a civilian president actually taking office in early 1958. He was overthrown in the early 1960s and somebody else took over; then again there was a legal election and the victor in turn was overthrown. Argentina now has a military government of corporate ideology and quasiliberal economic persuasion. This series of breakdowns reflects the inability of the Argentines to integrate their own "blackheads," which is what they call lower-class Peronistas. The term in Argentina is *cabecita negra*, which refers not to Negroes, but to persons with a mestizo appearance because they tend to come from the hinterland where intermarriage took place in past centuries.

By defining "nation" in this way, it is quite clear that there are no true international relations in Latin America. Where there are no social nations, there can be intergovernmental relations, but not truly inter*national* ones in a substantive sense. This conclusion leads to another question, how to organize conceptually the relations between a powerful nation-state, like the United States, and the varying kinds of traditional non-national situations of Latin America. To dignify this relation with a notion of juridical equality is conceptual folly, as can be indicated by returning to the earlier two cases.

### Effect on American Foreign Policy

In 1945 a peculiar government began to evolve in Guatemala in which the elite group increasingly became verbal Marxists. The constitution of the republic did not reflect Marxism, nor did the laws or most political practice, but the words indeed did. For example, the government newspaper began to follow the Moscow line, and germ warfare propaganda pictures against the U.S. presence in Korea were officially circulated. This tendency naturally alarmed the United States, and as was admitted in a public speech by President Kennedy, and as had been earlier admitted by Secretary of State Dulles, the United States intervened in Guatemalan affairs in 1954. The way we did it was to organize a small cadre of exiled Guatemalans (300 or so), supply them, train them, give them some money and a few airplanes, and turn them loose—and the government of Arbenz fell, panic-stricken before the great implicit power of the United States. I do not know who was more surprised, the leader of the insurgent forces or Mr. Dulles, but in any event the Arbenz government fell. Not that any Guatemalans inside the country took up arms to oppose it or to defend it; the government simply fell in the face of what was little more than a clenched fist. There were a few engagements and some people were killed, but it was a bush-league operation. The revolution was cheap and successful.

Another country, that other one I have described, found itself with a government also disliked by the United States and, even worse, instead of being merely verbally Marxist, it also became legally and actually Marxist, worst of all, it moved into the cold war. The United States thought that if intervention of this indirect type worked in one place, it would work in another. A replication was undertaken. This time we could not use Honduras, Nicaragua, and Panama as easily as before, but we did set up training camps in Guatemala and other Central American countries, and recruiting was carried out in Florida and New Orleans. We were going to send another cadre of refugees into a Latin country and cause a government to fall.

So it was that we bought ourselves the Bay of Pigs, based on the utter inability to recognize that if Cuba is only ninety miles from Florida, then Florida is only ninety miles from Cuba—in short, that Cuba is a highly Americanized country. From 1898 on, social reforms had destroyed village culture on the island. The American presence turned Cuba into a class society, not a color-caste society; it broke traditional organization, laced the island with communications, and created a group of persons mobilized and thus ready to be integrated into national community. Cuba had shaken loose the old, but lower-class Cubans by the 1950s had not yet been given institutionalized access to and participation in the institutions of the modern national society.

Castro did not have to be a political genius to survive. All he had to be was nationalist—and that indeed he was. What had saved him, as he himself said in public speeches, was his most powerful weapon, the ability to raise the price of an invasion by throwing a citizens' army into combat. There is a difference—not perhaps in a moral sense, but certainly politically and symbolically—between six hundred deaths, as is the estimated figure in Guatemala in 1954, and an unknown number of dead persons, allegedly estimated variously by military persons as possibly between 100,000 and 500,000 for a successful Cuban invasion. Certainly one reason that Mr. Kennedy stopped the Bay of Pigs operation is that he suddenly realized he did not have the vaguest idea of how many casualties might be incurred if he moved American military forces into the island. Nobody could really have known, for there was no way of estimating how many Cubans would put themselves in a position to be killed in order to defend their government. Mr. Kennedy could not have known; but Mr. Eisenhower's advisors based their estimates on prenational Guatemalan society, where casualties were very low.

But what happens in an early type of national war? How are effects to be estimated when fighting not a few soldiers and politicians, but when a semimobilized protonational population is involved? I have often listened with bitter amusement to those who say we could have won—all we had to do was send in the Air Force. Of course, one can win almost any entirely military operation by sending in the Air Force, assuming the enemy is not a rocket-nuclear power. We could even "win" the war in Vietnam this way. All we have to do is to use big enough bombs, and we certainly have them. But the political point of the exercise is to have enough left after military victory to have made the game worth it. The point is also to be able to pursue the controversy within limits that do not break the consensual patterns which give our own national society its coherence.

In the United States we are suffering from a threat of the opposite kind, from the possible dissolution of national consensus. Those young persons who will no longer answer those frank letters of "Greetings" are, in effect, withdrawing their tacit consent from the society. They are saying that the patterns overlying the divisions in which they find themselves make it impossible for them to maintain their position inside the polity. Politically they are taking a very old-fashioned Lockean position, saying that their natural rights are being violated, that the social compact is broken. Such withdrawal, if wholesale, is obviously the most profoundly subversive threat to a national society that can be advanced against it, a breakdown of the ordering synthesis of modern life.

One must then ask the question, for Latin America as well as for the United States: what are the limits of national cohesion? How much national cohesion is a good thing? And when does the medicine turn into poison? This question is one of the most fundamental in political theory, but the mere necessity of posing it in real situations always signals great social danger.

In summary, race in Latin America is usually a function of class and culture. An Indian, mestizo, or Negro is within the spectrum of humanity, not an alien creature. However, most Latin American countries have failed to develop national communities, not allowing the lower classes, which group roughly along color lines, access to the national institutions. The consequent lack of national cohesion has resulted in the inability of these countries effectively to defend their national interests, whether military, economic, or even cultural. The effects on and implications for the foreign policy of the United States, a strong national community as well as a mighty military power, are necessarily very great.

# 7

# The Growth of
# Counterracism among
# New African Polities

*George W. Shepherd, Jr.*

## I

Paradoxically, with the triumph of nationalism in much of Africa, racism is spreading into regions and among groups where it was never present before as a major social force. Note that what we are concerned with here is not simply a growing "race consciousness" among Africans but a *racism*. Racism is based on distinctions between groups in terms of inherent physical, psychological, and spiritual qualities. Such racist attitudes often result in overt prejudice and hostility between groups and polities. They also lead to the establishment of racist systems of stratification between dominant and subordinate racial groups within and between nations.[1]

Ethnocentricism is closely related to racism: hostile attitudes between ethnic groups very easily become magnified where even superficial physical differences exist. The inferior/superior presumptions of ethnocentrism are as relative and unscientific as racial physical criteria have been for cleavage distinctions within societies.

Thus the racial conflicts of Africa are by no means limited

to the black-white syndrome. Racial hostilities with an ethno-centric origin have increasingly led to violence in Africa today, between Somali and Amharic, African and Arab, Bantu and Nilote, to mention only a few conflicts of less notoriety than the confrontation in southern Africa between Bantu and Afri-kaner.

Racism is spreading in two directions in Africa. The first direction is a growing black versus white confrontation over southern Africa. Many of the new African states, especially in West Africa, where there never has been in the past a deep white versus black schism, are developing a racist attitude. In the second direction are the racial ethnocentric conflicts where, with the withdrawal of the restraining forced unity of colonialism, ancient enmities emerge into prominence.

These two directions interact upon each other. The ethno-centric conflict weakens basic African unity in its attempts to deal with black-white conflicts like Rhodesia. And in turn, the black-white hostility creates a convenient scapegoat for African leaders who face internal problems of disunity and conflict with neighboring African states.

Most African leaders, like Tammany Hall Irish politicians, will not admit publicly their dependence on racial ethnocentric politics. They learned their lessons from the colonial period with its ethnocentric racist doctrine of "the civilizing mission" brought to Africa by settlers, missionaries, and colonial admin-istrators.

Particularly tragic is the failure of the universal spirit that pervaded so much of early African nationalism to find fulfill-ment in the triumphs of national independence. This aspiration was well expressed by Julius Nyerere when he said:

> The Challenge of the twentieth century is the conversion of na-tionalism into internationalism. Our success depends on whether we have the courage to place our trust in world institutions of which we each are such a small part, and whether the leaders of

nation states will lead in the direction of unity on the basis of equality.[2]

Greater recognition of the nature of racial politics may help restore the goals of equality and justice. And social science has much it can contribute to this understanding.


## II

The basic spirit of negritude of the French writers Aime Césaire and Leopold Senghor was a Negro culture-race consciousness and not a doctrine of racism.[3] When Sartre called negritude "anti-racist-racism," he was not aware of the careful attempts of Senghor and Antoine Diop to eliminate all allusion to physical and noncultural distinctions between the races.[4] They sought to project the significance of the African's contribution to world civilization, not his superiority.

The same spirit can be found in the English-speaking Africans' view of the African personality. According to Nkrumah and Nyerere, African political ideas of democracy and socialism were derived from a past of African tribal communalism. For the African, these systems were superior to those brought and imposed by the West. Yet ethnocentric views were avoided because no allusion to Africa's superior intelligence or morality was implied.

This race consciousness sweeping through African literature and political thought has more recently been challenged by African intellectuals such as B. A. Ogot, historian at the University College of Nairobi. Professor Ogot feels that excessive emphasis on race and culture by African intellectuals has led to an "inverted racism" in which Africans are looking for distinctive qualities much as European intellectuals and politicians did earlier. Says Professor Ogot, "The fact is there is no African mind distinct from the common human mind. And although there may be a difference in their contents and products, this social heritage into which they entered will be due primarily to differences in the culture and have nothing at all to do with the colour of one's skin."[5]

This "inverted racism" in negritude has also been criticized by Ezekiel Mphahlele and Franz Fanon as based on imaginary rather than real differences. In the main, differences of view follow an English versus a French-speaking viewpoint. The strong assimilationist pressures of French colonial policy, plus the close relations maintained with independent French-speaking states, may have produced a desire to express identity through distinctive qualities. "Inverse racism" seems a harsh term to apply to negritude. But where negritude provides an intellectual rationale for the more ethnocentric political phenomenon of counterracism, a much more serious development must be considered.

Counterracism or ethnocentric nationalism is, in fact, a growing political mood on the African continent. In the main, it is a reaction against the persistence of white supremacist systems in southern Africa. White supremacy is not a phenomenon discussed here because its extent and power have been well-documented elsewhere. It should be said, however, that the assertion by Rhodesians that Africans cannot rule themselves in less than fifty years is a racialist assumption in the modern world. Rhodesia's African tribal kinsmen in Zambia, immediately to the north, are ruling themselves with effective results. What the Rhodesians, Portuguese, and South Africans are doing by their refusal to grant political rights to Africans is to preserve the interests of a racial minority. This denial is built on the feeling of racial solidarity of the whites against the blacks, backed with the force of the state. The greater the force necessary to keep Africans from exercising equal rights, the more intensive the racist feelings of the white minority. South Africa is a police state imposing its apartheid doctrine on the Africans. Much has been made of alleged nonracist attitudes of the Portuguese. But social acceptance of "assimilados" is not a substitute for self-rule. The denial of this principle today except in the most remote and undeveloped regions is an ethnocentric form of racism.

Counterracism has been present in the black versus white nature of the anticolonial struggle from the beginning. Peter Abrahams' vivid description of the undercurrent of feeling at a pan-African meeting in England in the 1940's was well symbolized by Udomo's impassioned speech and the words to the English present in the hall.[6] More explicit were some of the oaths taken by Mau Mau recruits in Kenya.

This counterracist mood seemed to soften after the initial success of nationalism. However, the frustrations of liberationist leaders who have watched their dreams fade have produced a new hard line. Africa is not unified and there has been no quick victory over the Portuguese, Rhodesians, and South Africans. The strength of white supremacy is attributed to the complicity of the white Western world in sustaining the white supremists in power in Rhodesia, Mozambique, Angola, and South Africa. A conspiracy of the white race and of Western interests is frequently believed to underlie public professions of policies of opposition to these regimes. Thus an attitude of white racialism invites the counterracial view of black solidarity of a Mau Mau movement in Kenya or a Kibandi or Simba movement in the Congo. These views are based on mythical assumptions, but their sociological and pathological origins are to be found in the realities of African life.

Certain contemporary conflicts have illuminated the growth of counterracist attitudes, particularly in the Congo and Rhodesian crises. Among the more radical African states these feelings were inflamed by the Stanleyville drop of Belgian paratroopers by American planes operating from a British base in November 1965. Most Africans interpreted this as direct

interventionary action on behalf of the unpopular Moise
Tshombe government, as the use of South African mercenaries
by Tshombe had already inflamed racial feelings. Debate at the
United Nations was heated. The Foreign Minister of the Congo
(Brazzaville), Charles-David Ganuo, opened the December
General Assembly debate with these words:

> When we were young we learned that in music, one white was
> worth two blacks. The infamous humanitarian operation of Stan-
> leyville has now proved to us that a white, especially if his name
> is "Carlson" or if he is an American, a Belgian, or an Englishman
> is worth thousands upon thousands of blacks.[7]

Such statements led the British historian B. C. Sutcliffe to
comment that "despite the grain of truth in his protestations,
the deep feeling in many of the African speeches was coloured
by a hue of apparent antiwhitism." [8] Adlai Stevenson, the
American delegate to the U.N. at the time, charged he "had
never before heard such irrational, irresponsible, insulting, and
repugnant language used in the chambers of the United Nations," and that "the antidote for white racism is not black
racism." [9]

Similarly, with regard to the Rhodesian crisis, it is widely
believed in Africa that the real reason the British government
has not acted with force against the illegal Smith government
has been the sense of white solidarity between Englishmen and
Rhodesians. "If the rebels had been black, force would have
been used," an African foreign office official stated flatly to me.
Thus an article in *Crisis and Change,* an organ of southern
African exiles, accused Wilson of "a cynical betrayal."

African attitudes toward Great Britain for the British failure
to use force have been marked by emotion and intemperate
actions. In voting to withdraw diplomatic recognition of the
U.K., the Council of Ministers of the OAU took a stand they
could not carry through. As it was, only nine actually severed

relations and most of these soon restored them when they saw the majority had not complied. While there is a certain realism in African states exerting pressure on the British, withdrawal of recognition only hurt those who did it and had no effect on Britain. This kind of extreme and inappropriate action arises from an emotional frustration over their own weakness and inability to intervene directly themselves.

In a letter analyzing the dangers of a race war replacing the cold war in the Afro-Asian world, Margaret Legum saw three broad trends: "first, the sense of solidarity between the peoples subjected to centuries of oppression and humiliation—largely a matter of colour; second, antiimperialism, which is both a political and an emotional movement—largely anti-Western; third, the international unity of the have-nots to redress the balance of the haves—which could be described as an international class war." [10]

Mrs. Legum also pointed to another new source of friction—Communist China. As the Indian political scientist V. P. Dutt has stressed, China is prone to play upon her non-Western and colored identity with Africa. This takes the form of reminding the Africans, "We were also regarded by the imperialist aggressors as a so-called 'inferior race.' " [11] Since China is almost the only great power willing to supply the means the southern Africans need for their liberation struggle, they find an attentive audience.

While all these factors and China's influence explain a great deal about counterracialism, they should not detract from the overriding reality of the aggravation of white dominance in southern Africa. This system is still linked closely to the Western world. While we deplore it in official statements, a broad flow of economic, military, and scientific cooperation continues to strengthen it against growing African fury.

Professor Irving Louis Horowitz, reflecting on some of the consequences of colonialism, reminds us that in situations of rapid development, Western responsibility for implanting racial mental attitudes among dependent peoples was primary:

> If the mental set of developing man appears to us to be excessively focused on feelings of inferiority based on racial differences, we must remember that the highly developed societies have brought this racialism down on themselves through their own peculiar notions of superiority. The marks of oppression remain implanted on the "liberated" peoples of the Third World, but in some measure this is because the habits of the oppressor remain implanted on the peoples of the "enlightened" First and Second Worlds.[12]

### III

As indicated at the outset, the racial problems of Africa cannot be understood merely within the context of the black versus white syndrome. With colonial power no longer holding together vast areas and disparate peoples who have fought each other for centuries, another dimension to Africa's racial troubles has emerged.

Professors Coleman and Rosberg, in their book, *National Integration and Political Parties in Tropical Africa*, have demonstrated clearly that the major problem of African stability and unity is closely related to ethnic differences. As suggested earlier, it would be very misleading to imply that all ethnic rivalries and hostilities have a racial character. Most of the tribal hostilities of Africa can be attributed primarily to differences arising from methods of subsistence, religious worship, and authority systems generally known as culture. However, when racial and cultural differences merge, hostility seems to be intensified into a cultural racism based on ethnocentricism.

Although much of the racial feeling of difference between groups is ethnocentric in origin, there frequently are real physical differences. Africa is a continent of considerable variety in racial characteristics. None of these racial groups are pure but perhaps the poor communications system and vast terrain have preserved distinctive physical characteristics more completely than on other continents. Anthropologists disagree about the exact number of racial groups and their division because of the extensive mixing, but Herskovits speaks of four major African subtypes in tropical Africa, and a fifth in North Africa.[13]

Intermingling between racial groups has gone on over the centuries, such as the Negro absorption of the Khoisan "brown men" of central and southern Africa. In some cases assimilation has succeeded in virtually eradicating any significant racism, as between the Berbers and Arabs of the Maghreb. However, modern times have unfortunately witnessed the outbreak of a number of cases of inter-African racism, frequently spilling over into communal violence and interstate war. One of the most bloody has been the massacre of the Watutsi (Nilo-Sudanic) in Burundi by their former slaves, the Bahutu (Negrillo-Bantu). Conservative estimates put the number of Watutsi that have been killed in the thousands and at least 50,000 have fled into neighboring Uganda for sanctuary. In Zanzibar during the revolution of early 1964, the ancient antagonisms between the mainland Africans and the land-owning Arabs erupted and led to the overthrow of the Arab-dominated Zanzibar National party by the African-dominated Afro-Shirazi party, which seized the clove plantations amid much bloodshed. Racial feelings here became confused with strong ideological as well as cultural differences.

In Uganda the division between the northern "Nilotes," as they are called by the Baganda and the southern and western "Bantu," appears to be growing. Several well-educated Baganda have expressed the belief that there are racial as well as cultural differences between the two groups. The alleged racial differences have a most tenuous basis in perceivable differences but the race-consciousness associated with them has become sufficiently widespread to be the basis of real political cleavage. President Obote's abolition of the constitution and seizure of power in 1966 is attributable to these differences. Thus political differences in 1966 between the ruling Uganda Peoples Congress and the opposition group, Kabaka Yekka, were intensified by strong racial feelings.

On the horn of Africa, there has been no peace since Somalia became independent in 1960 because of the strength of Somali irredentism which directs itself against Ethiopia and Kenya. In both the RFD of Kenya and the Agaden of Ethiopia, the conflict has strong racist undertones. There is also a Hamitic influence among the Somali and a Nilotic and Negro strain among the Kikuyu which aggravates the Moslem-Christian dichotomy of these groups.

By far the most complex and difficult problem of racial-culture conflict I have encountered in Africa is in the southern Sudan. This is again essentially a cultural conflict but has stronger racial sources than any of the other examples cited. The major ethnic groups of the Sudan are the Arab Hamites of the north, the Negro Bantu of the southern borders, and the Nilotes farther down the Nile. Only slightly more than half the population of the Sudan speaks Arabic (as a first language). The western Sudan, especially the Baggara and Nuba mountain peoples, represents a fascinating blend of Arab and African. But, despite the dominance of the southern Sudan by Arab-speaking peoples for well over a hundred and fifty years, Islam and the Arab way of life have penetrated only the fringe of the three provinces of the south—Equatoria, Upper Nile, and Bahr el Ghazal.

During the rise of modern nationalism in the Sudan in the 1950's and 1960's, the Africans of the south were, with few exceptions, outside the major movements. During the 1950s, the major request was for a federal status to secure their African way of life from the Arab. However, with the removal of the British colonial presence, African ethnic expression took an increasingly violent turn. Under the period of military rule from 1958–64, the separationist movement and the Anya Nya insurgency campaign began and appears to have grown in strength. This trend continued even after the restoration of political party rule in November 1964.

The causes of this bitter ethnic conflict, though far too complex to detail here, can be traced back to the Muhammed Ali period of the slave trade. Its roots can be found in the separate development policy of the British and in the attitudes of missionaries who believed that Christianity was engaged in a great race with Islam for the souls of southern Sudanese.

But the concern of this paper is with the racial factors and these have been and are strongly present. There has been little social interchange between African and Arab Sudanese over the decades. I observed that the social life of the southern student at the University of Khartoum was almost entirely separate from the northern students. Yet the attitude there of mutual tolerance was far ahead of what was faced by the average southern laborer on the streets of Omdurman and Khartoum.

The African sense of alienation from the Arab way of life has gone very far. This was most vehemently expressed by Joseph Oduho, the president of the Azania Liberation Front, in terms that clearly had a racial undertone, "No Arab can be trusted to keep his word," and so on. Among the northern-educated Arab elite I did not encounter such overt racial feeling. However, there have been many accounts of the behavior of northern troops in the civil conflict showing disregard for the importance of African life. There are moderates on both sides who believe that African and Arab can build together a united Sudan but they have so far been voices crying in the wilderness.

Ethnocentric racial conflicts of this kind, more than any other single factor, are apt to be the source of serious conflicts and even wars between the African states of the future.

## Policy Implications for the United States

Several general policy implications emerge from this interpretation of counterracism and ethnocentricism on the African continent. While the United States is not widely regarded in Africa as a colonial power, it is increasingly viewed with suspicion because of the racism Africans see in American society. This has not been offset by official American pronouncements of support of constitutional principles of equality or even recent legal and social reform at home. Our increasing difficulties with the American black community are linked by them to white imperialistic ambitions toward colored races in the world. Unfortunately for the United States, the Vietnam fiasco has greatly heightened these doubts about the integrity of American equalitarian goals. There are, of course, many African leaders who do not have this simplistic view of American society and foreign policy but they are increasingly hindered in expressing their difference by the growth of popular suspicions concerning United States racial imperialism.

As might be expected, this suspicion often contributes to the growth of what I have called a counterracialist reaction whenever direct intervention takes place in African affairs. Events such as the Stanleyville drop are seen from an entirely different perspective in Africa than they are in the West. Any attempt to use American power, particularly military power, automatically triggers strong accusations of racial neocolonialism at many levels in African society. While this was most strikingly represented by the more radical leaders such as Kwame Nkrumah during his reign in Ghana, the sentiment is shared on a broad basis throughout Africa.

Skillful communist efforts in Africa to play upon these

attitudes have frequently been successful. Thus racial feelings are a highly exploitable element in cold war terms. This in itself should be enough to create extreme caution on the part of American policy-makers in their use of interventionary power in Africa.

However, a negative policy of withdrawal cannot resolve the problem. Positive steps by the United States to demonstrate clearly to Africans that United States power is used on behalf of the interests of justice and African self-determination is the surest way to counteract the trend. Speeches at the United Nations or by traveling dignitaries are not convincing. Only actual steps can produce a change. The areas where this would be most effective are in southern Africa. Here the United States is widely believed to be indirectly supporting the Portuguese, Rhodesians, and South Africans. A major reversal of military and economic relations with these countries would certainly convince many doubters concerning the sincerity of U.S. support for social justice in the world. Some of the practical steps that might be taken are referred to in John Marcum's essay. Such sweeping changes could only be introduced provided the U.S. policy-makers become convinced of the dangers implicit within the current trends and sought new priorities. Whether this can be done without a major change in terms of racial justice on the domestic scene is open to question. But clearly the two reforms are closely linked.

The temptations to intervene in Africa are apt to grow in direct proportion to the increasing instability of African polities themselves. As has been noted, the racial and ethnocentric conflicts among Africans are increasing. There is little evidence that the horrors of the Nigeria-Biafra war will immediately institute the social reforms and tolerance of differences necessary to avert such crises elsewhere in Africa. Widespread instability of governments and increasing conflict among ethnocentric and racial groups may well be the price that African societies will pay for rapid social change over the next several years.

Outside powers such as the United States can do little to prevent these hostilities, but they can do a great deal to reduce their intensity and duration. They should refrain from intervention and seek international agreements to maintain this status. The supply of arms and the participation of mercenaries is the most important aspect to limit. As the Middle East has clearly shown, the intervention of great powers only intensifies and prolongs conflict. The way out is not simple or easy. But the alternative would be a frightening one indeed: a multitude of insoluble Arab-Israeli conflicts involving mass starvation and continuous terrorism which periodically threaten to involve the world in conflagrations over issues that are tangled and half-forgotten in the past of ancient enmities.

## NOTES

1. This interpretation is based on the UNESCO study, *The Race Question in Modern Science* (Paris: UNESCO, 1968).

2. Julius K. Nyerere. *Freedom and Unity* (London: Oxford University Press, 1967), p. 284.

3. See Aime Césaire in Lilyan Kesteloot, *Les écrivains noir de langue française: naissance d'une littérature*, 2nd ed. (Bruxelles: Univ. libro de Bruxelles, 1965).

4. Walter Skurnik, "Leopold Sedar Senghor and African Socialism", *Journal of Modern African Studies* (November 1965): 352.

5. Ogot, "Racial Consciousness among Africans," *East Africa Journal*, April 1965, p. 23.

6. Peter Abrahams, *A Wreath for Udomo* (London: Faber, 1956).

7. United Nations Document S/PV 1170, p. 66.

8. "The Racial Issue at the United Nations: A Study of the

African States Reaction to the American Belgian Congo Rescue Operation of 1964," *International Relations,* 2, no. 12 (October 1965): 837.

9. *UN Monthly Chronicle,* 2 (January 1965): 13.

10. Letters to the Editor, *Crisis and Change* (November, December 1965): 4.

11. V. P. Dutt, *China and the World* (New York: Praeger, 1966), p. 273.

12. Irving Louis Horowitz, *Three Worlds of Development* (New York: Oxford University Press, 1966), pp. 331–2.

13. M. Herskovits, *The Human Factor in Changing Africa* (New York: Knopf, 1962), pp. 33–34.

# 8 Race in Africa: United States Foreign Policy

*Rupert Emerson*

The question of race relations, both domestic and international, has of late thrust itself more and more upon our attention as one of inescapably vital concern to us, cutting deeply into many aspects of our lives and determining our future. This question raises fighting issues everywhere, and stirs animosities which threaten peace at home and friendly relations with peoples abroad.

On the international scene, the United States nowhere confronts a situation potentially more laden with racial tensions and dangers than those involved in its relations with Africa. Given the multiplication of African states, the challenge to the rest of the world posed by white-dominated southern Africa, and the upsurge of the Black Power and Black Nationalism movements in the United States, African-American relations present in many ways a clear case of racial confrontation. It is also true that the more deeply one penetrates into those relations and their implications, the more subtle and complex some of the major issues become. To cite a single example,

the international ramifications of race relations become apparent when it is remembered that black American athletes at
the Olympic Games in Mexico City attracted some measure
of world attention by asserting their black identity. Prior to
the games, the readmission of South Africa stirred up a global
furor, involving the threat of a boycott by some thirty-six
countries, which in due course brought about the withdrawal
of the invitation to South Africa on the ground that its
apartheid doctrine and practices were incompatible with the
basic principles which the games sought to promote.

Let me state at the outset two central themes which are very
obvious but which need to be set forth clearly on the record.
On the African side, in the last decade and a half virtually
all of Africa has become independent except that vitally important area, the huge block of southern Africa. There has been
a multiplication of independent African states, coming to independence much more quickly than anyone expected, and by
the end of 1968, numbering forty-one. On this side of the
Atlantic, in a movement obscurely but indisputably related
to this drive toward independence, some 22 million or more
of the population of the United States are people who are of
African descent. They also, quite clearly, are in quest of independence, whether it is in the sense of full integration into
the broader American society, or of Black Nationalism, or
perhaps even of a return to Africa.

On both sides, in Africa and in the United States, there is
a far greater awareness than there was before of the existence
of these two great communities, and also, I am afraid, a much
greater awareness that on both sides of the Atlantic, race and
wealth or poverty are almost synonymous. On the whole,
it is the white peoples who constitute the affluent societies. It
is the black people generally who are poor and underdeveloped
or, in this country, less educated, less employed, and at a lower
level of economic life. That again, now well documented in

the public record, inevitably establishes a tie, although what one is to make of this closer knowledge of each other and their respective positions in the world is, I think, one of the debatable issues.

I am firmly of the opinion that there is no major part of the world to which the United States pays less attention and assigns a lower priority than Africa. It is a continent of marked concern to the United States only when special crises break out, particularly crises involving any kind of communist threat, as, for example, in the Congo after its independence in 1960. If Africa is of relatively small concern to the United States, it is surely also true that the Negro attitude in the United States toward Africa has only a marginal bearing on American policy there. The Negroes are obviously a highly significant minority in this country, but they are a minority, and still have relatively slight political influence, even if it is growing. To put it in crude terms, there is no reason to assume that anybody can deliver a sufficiently substantial Negro vote on African issues to affect the outcome of significant elections. The primary Negro concern inevitably is domestic in character and only incidentally focused on African matters. Insofar as Afro-Americans vote in a bloc they will vote for a Negro candidate or an issue more directly concerning the Negro community than far-distant African affairs.

What then is the Negro attitude toward Africa, or rather where does the Negro stand on Africa? This is perhaps an absurd question because quite obviously there is no single Negro attitude, no single Negro position, in relation to Africa, and furthermore attitudes are changing, subtle, and complex in various ways. The relation of the Negro American community to Africa is multifaceted, and inevitably hazardous to try to summarize.

The treatment to which African slaves were subjected after their arrival here largely caused them to forget where they came from in memory. There was soon no specific point of origin, either tribal or geographical, to which they could look back. Further, the countries from which they came could not have been the present Nigeria or Sierra Leone or the Congo because these colonial creations were not then in existence. At all events their source of origin has been lost as the decades and centuries have gone by, with the result that their identification with Africa is necessarily, in that respect, loose and amorphous, although it may, of course, be none the less passionately felt and find its expression in some more generalized guise such as Pan-Africanism or negritude.

Certainly for the last century and more, there has been sporadic but growing contact between the Negro community in this country and Africa, especially in the earlier phases through churches, through missions, and through African students who were brought to this country to study in Negro schools or colleges that were almost always church-affiliated. As George Shepperson has put it:

> It was to be the connexion between the Negro churches of America and Africa which, after the Civil War, was to provide a channel for increasing numbers of Africans to gain an education in coloured American schools and colleges. . . . The phenomenon of "Ethiopianism" in South Africa went back to 1896-8 when separatist South African churches had sought affiliation with the pioneer Negro American independent church, the African Methodist Episcopal Church, and its fiery Bishop, H. M. Turner, had made his trip to Africa. Through such connexions, numbers of Africans from South Africa were to visit the United States, often in search of an education which seemed to them easier to obtain in Negro American colleges than at home.[1]

At the present time Negro Americans in substantial numbers are constantly going to Africa or returning from it, frequently still on church business, but now for many other purposes as well, as witness the African travels of Negro businessmen, government employees, and educators, and also of such public figures as Malcolm X and Stokely Carmichael. Similarly, wholly unprecedented numbers of Africans visit the United States on governmental business in Washington or at United Nations headquarters in New York, as students or members of conferences, and in many other capacities.

Despite these constantly expanding contacts, the Negro community has suffered, and continues to suffer, from a widespread ignorance of Africa. It is also noteworthy that much of the Negro community has had a considerable distaste for the assumption of an association with Africa, which has traditionally been portrayed as a primitive or savage continent. Everyone is familiar with the cartoons that used to appear from time to time not long ago depicting Africans dancing about the boiling pot into which the missionary was about to be plunged. Malcolm X writes that although his father was a follower of Marcus Garvey and spoke of Africa for the Africans, he himself in his childhood never thought of black people in Africa: "My image of Africa, at that time, was of naked savages, cannibals, monkeys and tigers, and steaming jungles." That is not the kind of picture with which a rising people here want to associate themselves. Incidentally, both here and in Africa, it is held as a grievance against the whites that this is the picture of Africa which whites have come to take for granted and been prepared to broadcast to the world. The effect until fairly recently, and no doubt for many still, has been an effort to evade any stress on African origins precisely because black Africa was so habitually portrayed as a part of the world which civilized men looked down on. That attitude has been changing as more knowledge of Africa has become available. Now there is a sense of pride in the independent African states and in the African role in the United Nations and other international conferences and organizations. Where blackness used to be scorned, now it is loudly proclaimed: people have come to be proud of the fact that they are black and share in a black heritage. In part, of course, sentiments such as these find their most vigorous expression in the Black Power and Black Nationalist movements.

There has always been some impulse or pressure to return to Africa from the diaspora. At an early stage in the last century, a drive was undertaken to secure the return particularly of liberated slaves to Africa, establishing them in what came to be Liberia, as the British similarly developed Sierra Leone, but it was not a movement which won favor among the freed slaves themselves in this country. The high point of agitation for a return to Africa came at the end of World War I in the movement led by Marcus Garvey to whose influence Kwame Nkrumah paid high tribute—a movement which spread the gospel of return vividly and dramatically, but had virtually no effect in bringing Negroes back to Africa. At no point, in fact, has there been more than a trickle of emigration of Negroes to Africa, and I think it unlikely that there will be any great increase in migration in the foreseeable future.

Some of the present issues concerning the position of the Negroes in relation to Africa and to this country can be symbolized by the names applied to them in the United States. The principal designation for a long time was "American Negro," which laid its emphasis on the special Negro element. We do not speak of an American Italian or an American Irishman; if we did, we would presumably be singling out an American who was or had been in this country but continued to be essentially Italian or Irish. The phrase which is used is always Italian American, Irish American, Polish American. More recently, the swing has been in that direction to the term "Negro American," reversing the two words, and putting the emphasis on his American character, thus placing the

Negro in the same position as other ethnic communities which have been integrated into the overall American family. Now, certainly among the younger, more militant groups of Negroes, the turn is sharply against the use of the term "Negro" which is regarded as inherently derogatory and designed only to indicate the inferior position of the black man in the American society. The current trend is to use either the term "black" or, perhaps, "Afro-American," both bringing the African connection to the fore, the latter retaining the American link. Both are terms used by the militants who are demanding that the Negro community undertake its own separate development, thus producing, in an unhappy but inevitable association of terms, its own doctrine and practice of racialism and apartheid.

This is both an immensely interesting, and in many ways an ominous turn of events. It represents repudiation of integration and assimilation stemming from a total distrust of the white man and any collaboration with him, and is reflected in a contemptuous attitude toward the civil-rights movement, democracy, and the vote, as all being things which really do not contribute anything of basic significance to the Negro. It is contended that the Negro must fight for himself and through Black Power achieve the consolidation and identification of his own community as a separate entity—all of which, of course, fits in with the striking report of February 1968 by the President's Advisory Committee on Civil Disorders, holding that our nation is moving toward a division into two societies, one black, one white, separate and unequal. The militants among the blacks are prepared to accept and strive toward precisely this goal of two separate communities of black and white, but also, of course, they want, at least in the first rounds, not only to complete and strengthen black separateness but also to overcome the inequalities. The commission reported that these black militants "by preaching separatism unconsciously function as an accommodation to white racism." The Black

Nationalist with his insistence on Black Power represents a black racism which is the unhappy counterpart of the white segregationist, as it is also the response to him. The Black Muslim movement, now somewhat overshadowed by more recent and aggressive spokesmen and organizations, also fits into this pattern.

It appears to be the inevitable tendency of such movements to strengthen the significance of Africa for the Negro American. The more the Negro in this country repudiates the United States, the more he feels that he has no share in it and that the white man is not to be trusted to produce any benefits of value for the Negro community, the more he is likely to search for an alternative identity, an alternative and distinctive source of origin and present attachment. The natural tendency is to look to Africa as the homeland of the blacks from which he derives the new dignity and equality which he demands. A somewhat peculiar but easily comprehensible manifestation of this trend is found in the recent swing toward the teaching of Swahili. This is in its way an odd choice if it is taken as a restoration of historical cultural links because Swahili is an East African language while very few of the Negro-American population could have come from that part of the continent. But Swahili is sought out primarily as a symbolic gesture of identification with the African world, indicating less the renewal of a cultural heritage or the acquisition of a useful linguistic tool than something of a spiritual divorce from the American scene.

I would suggest that actually the same is true of much of the Negro interest in Africa. It is less a matter of identification with a real and concrete Africa than a symbolic identification with another continent, another people, to replace the attachment to the United States where the Negro militant feels he has been rejected. Negro Americans have a new pride in African achievements and in the independence of African states, although there must surely also be dismay at the political instability of so many of the states and their meager economic advance. Keen eyes watch out for any signs of race discrimination in American dealings with Africa, as in connection with the Belgian-American armed airborne intervention in 1964 at Stanleyville to rescue white hostages.

Black interest in Africa will inevitably increase, but as it stands now only a relatively few Negro Americans have any intimate knowledge of Africa, fewer still visit the continent, and only a tiny fraction of these settle there permanently. Very frequently one comes across the story of American Negroes who have gone to Africa in the hope of finding a welcome homeland, a people with whom they can immediately identify. Many have returned, discovering that they are far more American than they were aware of and that they are not really able to identify themselves with what turns out to be an alien community.[2]

It seems to me self-evident that failure on the part of white Americans to bring their fellow black Americans within the American family, or the refusal of Negroes to accept such integration, must greatly increase the likelihood that more and more of black America looks to Africa not only as a distant land of essentially symbolic importance representing a primarily mythical past, but also as a real flesh-and-blood continent in which full lives can be lived as they cannot in the United States. I take it for granted that the more the Negro American is accepted into the full American community, the less Africa is going to be of concern as anything very vitally touching his life, whatever his intellectual and sentimental interest in the continent. On the other hand, inability to achieve integration in this country must surely enhance Africa's charms, as a rise in anti-Semitism here would make Israel far more attractive to the Jewish American. Inevitably, there has already been some Negro effort to call on Africa to redress the imbalance of races in this country.

The distinguished Negro leader of the earlier part of the century, W. E. B. DuBois, returning from the Fifth Pan-African Congress in 1945, remarked, "We American Negroes should know that until Africa is free the descendents of Africa the world over cannot escape their chains." In other words, he already saw the Negro American as being linked to the independence and the dignity of the Africans in Africa. He called on the NAACP, of which he was one of the principal leaders, to put African freedom and the end of colonialism in the forefront of its program.

A later figure, Malcolm X, again a distinguished Negro leader, speaking of going to Africa and rather overrating Africa's political, economic, and strategic weight in the world, said that the Negroes would be out of their minds not to identify with the power bloc of the African nations which he saw as comprising at the international level the largest representative body and the largest force of any continent, in terms, of course, of the number of African states in the United Nations. "There is nothing," he said, "we couldn't accomplish if we secure our understanding and cooperation between the twenty-two million American Negroes and the African continent." In 1964 he attended the summit meeting of the Organization of African Unity in Cairo and appealed to the member states, all the free African states except South Africa, to bring before the UN as a matter of international concern, America's violation of human rights in dealing with its Negroes. The Organization of African Unity did in fact adopt a resolution on one side praising what had been going on in the civil-rights movement in the United States, on the other side calling for a much speedier end of all discrimination and segregation in this country. But, to the best of my knowledge, none of the African states has in fact ever brought before the United Nations the charge that the United States is violating any international agreements or the Human Rights Declaration or Covenants.

I have been speaking mainly of the contemporary militants, the largely younger militant groups, who undoubtedly wield increasing influence and quite possibly will be the dominant force from this time forward. But surely I must also mention another group of outstanding Negro citizens, older both in years and in their service as leaders in the African community, who have formed an organization called the American Negro Leadership Conference on Africa. Since 1962 this body has served both to shape and represent Negro opinion on Africa in order to bring pressure to bear on the government, to secure more acceptable policies for Africa, and to draw Negroes more fully into the State Department, into the Foreign Service, and into other agencies dealing with Africa and the world at large.

The people who have been central in the operation of the American Negro Leadership Conference are very familiar names such as Martin Luther King, A. Philip Randolph, Roy Wilkins, Whitney M. Young, Jr., James Farmer, Dorothy Haight, all of them representing a somewhat older and more moderate generation of Negro leaders. At its third biennial assembly in January 1967, in Washington, that conference dealt primarily with the issues of southern Africa, but it also urged larger aid programs for Africa, a greater enlistment of the American Negro community in all the activities dealing with Africa, and with a variety of other things including, for instance, urging the American trade union movement to expand, or at least to continue its activities, in helping to organize African labor.

In the spring of 1968, before the assassination of Martin Luther King, the *Los Angeles Times* of March 9, 1968 reported that this same organization had arranged to send a delegation of its leaders, including Dr. King, to Nigeria, in an effort to mediate between the federal government and secessionist Biafra. The newspaper account indicated that they would not have considered going had they not received some encouragement in Nigeria to believe that they could play a useful role in negotiating an end to the war. Although the mission ultimately fell through, it is an interesting manifestation of Negro American concern with Africa.

It is immensely useful to have an organization of this kind which builds up and mobilizes an informed public opinion on African questions. The United States is weak in its knowledge of Africa and in the pressure which groups dealing with African affairs can bring to bear. Not many people worry much about Africa, and relatively few other than the Negro community have any special reason to be concerned about that continent. In fact, Africa has been losing in attention in Washington in recent years. The high point of American concern with Africa, as Africans are well aware, was during the Kennedy administration. Africans still look back to the Kennedy administration as the one time when there was really an understanding of their problems in Washington and a readiness on the part of the Americans to collaborate both sympathetically and extensively. Since then, in part, of course, because of the overwhelming attention given our tragic involvement in Vietnam, the tendency has been to push Africa more into the background.

Turning to the other side of the picture, it is difficult to pin down the effect in Africa of the American racial situation and developments in any precise and meaningful fashion. The overall picture is obvious enough. The black Africans newly come to independence inevitably react with hostility to discrimination practiced against other black people overseas. They are shocked by the stories and the pictures of brutality, of murders, of bombings, of enforced segregation and ghettos. All the pictures that we see here are very likely to be played up in the African papers and to meet a sympathetic audience there. People who have just come out from under colonialism and bitterly resent the kind of white superiority that colonialism represented immediately respond sympathetically to similar, in some cases worse, practices against Negroes here.

There is, however, a very real ability, at least among the leaders in Africa, to distinguish between the position of the United States and the position of South Africa. The official policy toward which we have worked in the United States, however inadequately and slowly, is that we want to do away with segregation, that we want to integrate, to assimilate, to have a single American society, whereas South Africa, dominated by the Afrikaners, has taken precisely the other position. Its apartheid doctrine explicitly says that each racial community and even each African tribal community must have its own separate development, its own political organization, and run its own life in its own separate fashion. In the dominant white area of the country the Africans have no legitimate share whatsoever save as laborers in inferior, low-paid occupations, no general right of residence or of participation, no vote—in short, nothing to say in any part of the proceedings. That difference in basic principle between the United States and South Africa is clearly recognized; but it is also obvious that the longer desegregation takes and the more racial violence mounts, the less the expression by white Americans of honorable intentions toward their fellow Afro-Americans will be accepted at face value.

Unquestionably, there has been something of a draining away of the large store of good will toward the United States which existed in Africa, although this may not yet be a very significant matter. Insofar as African states have swung to the left, which is far from being generally the case, there is greater readiness to assume that the American white community is what the Black Power advocates say it is. An outstanding African liberation leader illustrated this by asserting (I merely cite this without further evidence as to its authenticity) that when Stokely Carmichael went to Africa he encountered rapt audi-

ences who were immediately taken by what he had to say
and assumed the validity of the positions he took. Yet when
Senator Edward Brooke of Massachusetts, a moderate Negro,
came to Africa, he was apparently met by puzzled confusion
or even hostility, as was indicated in a despatch from Nairobi
which commented on his inability to reach his audence as a
speaker there.

Since many other matters are inevitably involved, it is
almost impossible to estimate the precise significance of hostility to the American handling of its domestic racial problem
in the shaping of African private and official attitudes toward
the United States. If we must accept the proposition that
America's standing in Africa has declined, any number of issues
must be taken into account in seeking to explain the decline,
such as the Vietnam war to which Africans have generally
been hostile, the cutting back on aid funds, the downgrading
of Africa in American opinion, and specific American actions
or inactions in particular African places and situations, as in
relation to the Congo or Nigeria. A quite different kind of
issue which has damaged our relations with some countries
and peoples, notably those with strong Muslim affiliations, has
been American support of Israel, with its consequent impair-
ment of U.S. relations with North Africa and most Arab
countries.

On the whole, however, it may still be said that our relations
with most African countries remain at a reasonably friendly
level, even though with several of them relations are somewhat
indifferently amicable, or perhaps even merely indifferent,
rather than being in any sense close. Perhaps one cannot go
very much further than to say that mishandling of the race
problem at home opens the door to suspicions and grievances
that make life more difficult, but still do not as yet seriously
impair our ability to keep in touch with most African countries.
And yet certainly this is not an issue which we can pass by

casually and calmly. Former Secretary of State Rusk, speaking some years ago to a gathering of Negro leaders, said: "The biggest single burden that we carry on our backs in our foreign relations in the 1960's is the problem of racial discrimination at home." When the Secretary of State publicly so emphasizes our domestic racial crisis, it is evident that we still have far to go.

The most dangerous and difficult topic in our relations with Africa still remains to be discussed—the problem presented by the so-called white redoubt of southern Africa. This is the area in which adverse race relations most directly and most ominously appear. Here is to be found the gravest threat even though it may be that other areas will in fact explode well before Southern Africa boils over in such fashion as to command international attention. There may be other Congos, other Nigerias, into which we may be drawn to deal with particular situations, perhaps arising from the fact that Africa is itself so racially, or at least tribally, divided as to give its countries only a precarious hold on political stability and national identity.

Crises may erupt anywhere in Africa, but those which most gravely threaten a peaceful future, conceivably leading to World War III, have their roots in the racially bedeviled countries of southern Africa. The heart of the matter very simply is that while Africa north of the line marked by Rhodesia and the Portuguese territories has achieved independence, south of it white dominance remains. The areas involved include the large territories of Portuguese Angola and Mozambique, which remain unrepentantly colonial despite armed revolts that have imposed heavy financial and military burdens on Lisbon. Another Southern African country is Rhodesia, which laid down its unilateral declaration of independence (UDI) on November 11, 1965, citing a large part of the American Declaration of Independence, but omitting the key passages which affirm that all men are created equal and are endowed with certain inalienable rights, and that governments derive their just powers from the consent of the governed.

By any reckoning the center of Southern Africa is South Africa itself, by far the richest and most highly developed country on the continent, equipped with strong military and police forces, an effective political system, and an ability to supply most of its own needs with a decreasing reliance on the rest of the world. Its basic official policy is the doctrine of apartheid, which Africans universally reject with total disgust.

South Africa also controls and has virtually annexed the large territory of South-West Africa, which formally remains a mandate although barely a wisp of operative international jurisdiction over it has survived the passage of five decades and the disappearance of the League of Nations under whose auspices the mandate first came into being. In October 1967, in what appeared to be at least a futile, if not an actually undesirable, action, the UN General Assembly adopted a resolution which, in words, ousted South Africa from South-West Africa because of its apartheid doctrine, and announced that the United Nations was taking it over as an interim step toward independence. These were no doubt brave words but they ran head on into the fact that South Africa, which retains full control over the territory, has not the faintest intention of getting out, nor is the United Nations in a position to do anything about securing for its shadow government there the slightest thread of authority.

The list of Southern African countries is rounded out by mention of the three former High Commission territories, almost wholly embraced within South Africa, to which the British had retained title and which have now achieved independence under the names of Botswana, Lesotho, and Swaziland. In southern Africa only these three newly independent territories are black states, but they are in every respect so much within the control of South Africa that they can hardly expect to survive if they adopt policies which South Africa would regard as hostile. Their actual degree of independence presumably falls somewhere between that of Finland and the European satellites in relation to the Soviet Union.

As Africans see it, it is intolerable that the black states and peoples of the bulk of Africa, having won freedom from colonial rule, are now unable to do anything to achieve what they regard as the obviously inalienable right of the black majorities of South Africa, Rhodesia, and the rest of these white-dominated countries to take over and run their own affairs. They find themselves wholly frustrated by the fact that here, on their doorsteps, within an Africa whose unbroken unity they habitually proclaim, is an evil which they regard as the major evil of the world, but about which they can do little more than to issue denunciations, although guerrilla forces are now being increasingly mobilized. The white powers which might do something decisive about it are far from being persuaded that they should take the drastic steps many Africans advocate. It is the basic belief of the African leaders that only radical action, involving a full-scale boycott through compulsory sanctions across the board laid down by the Security Council, and quite probably intervention by force, can achieve the desired result of African majority rule. It is, however, clear on the record that the United States and its Western allies are not prepared to issue an all-out challenge to the countries of southern Africa and, as one good indicator of their reluctance, habitually work in the UN to soften resolutions rather than to press ahead more vigorously. Nor is there any reason to assume that the communist powers contemplate intervention.

Great Britain has nominal colonial jurisdiction over Rhodesia and vitally important investments in and trade with South Africa, the interruption of which would be likely to have grave consequences for the British economy and hence for Britain's ability to play its role as the major ally of the United States in a troubled world. Portugal as an American ally in NATO is supplied with arms which are not supposed to be used in its African colonial wars in Angola, Mozambique, and elsewhere, but which must in fact bolster the Portuguese military position. Washington's sharp and open criticism of Portuguese colonialism has not eliminated the general support which the United States has given Portugal, however much it may have irritated the Portuguese. Similarly, the United States has not concealed its distaste for South Africa's apartheid creed and did some years ago impose an arms embargo on the country, but it remains true both that the United States continues to be on friendly terms with South Africa and that the Americans have large, profitable, and growing investments in the country which is the most ardent advocate of white racialism. As far as Rhodesia is concerned, the United States has had only minimal political and economic involvement with the country. Washington has cooperated with the various calls for sanctions against Rhodesia since UDI, and appears generally to have aligned its policies closely with those of Britain. There is no evidence to indicate that the United States has been overly concerned about the failure of sanctions to bring down the rebel government in Salisbury, nor about the fact that oil has been pouring in, through Mozambique and South Africa, which is supplying and handling a good part of the Rhodesian trade above and under the counter.

South Africa is booming, South-West Africa remains under its sole control, Rhodesia is doing quite well, and the Portuguese colonies remain Portuguese colonies. The Africans accuse the United States and its allies of putting their economic interests ahead of the rights of oppressed human beings in southern Africa, and accuse the United States and Britain of putting their ties to "kith and kin" ahead of the indisputable rights of Africans. The United States, they protest, is ready to impose embargoes on trade and intercourse with China and Cuba and other communist countries but finds it impossible to take similar action against Portugal and South Africa. The United States will intervene by force in the Dominican Republic and in Vietnam but will not intervene by force against the white rebel regime of Ian Smith in Rhodesia or the Afrikaner apartheid regime in South Africa, nor will it aid in implementing by force the UN decision that South Africa's Mandate for South-West Africa has been terminated. As for Great Britain, the Africans point to the fact that the British have resorted to force in various other colonies, as in Guiana and Aden, and earlier in Kenya and Malaya when revolts broke out in those countries, but will not intervene by force against white rebels in Rhodesia.

Here inevitably American domestic failures in the racial sphere—the inability to make peace with the Negro community and to make the blacks a part of a single American society—come to be linked with American policies and problems in Africa. It is no arbitrary coincidence that all these things have happened together. The independence of the African states, the drive against white dominance in southern Africa, the civil-rights movement in this country, the rise of the black protest movement here, are all tied together as part of the fundamental racial ferment of the present day. As the black militants see it, the American failure to achieve more than tokenism either in southern Africa or in the United States is regarded as showing merely opposite sides of the same coin: in a few words, that the United States is not in fact prepared to do a job where black men are concerned. The Negro American sees the failures in southern Africa as confirmation of his growing loss of faith in the white man at home who balks at putting into effect the drastic reforms called for by the Kerner Commission on Civil Disorders and other similar bodies. The African likewise sees what goes on in Africa as the evident counterpart of the racial sins committed here.

How just are the charges and suspicions directed against the United States and its dominant white majority? In searching for the answer, another question or two may well be contemplated: are there in fact any circumstances under which the United States would intervene by force against the white rulers in any of the Southern African countries? Would we actually be prepared under presently foreseeable circumstances to intervene in any situation to safeguard the human rights of Africans or to establish the one-man, one-vote principle for which we claim to stand? Or, coming at the matter from the other side, how likely is it that we might find ourselves drawn into intervention if a violent African rising in, say, Rhodesia or South Africa were to cost the lives of many whites and threaten the lives of more? These are not easy questions, nor are there easy answers to them; but they are questions which Africans and Afro-Americans are sure to pose, and they believe that they know the answers to them, little as they may like the way they see the answers coming out.

I am myself by no means persuaded that we should presently intervene by force in any part of Africa under any circumstances which can now be foreseen, unless it were to participate in a police action which had overwhelming UN support. Among a number of other considerations, a matter of central importance is the immense difficulty—indeed, the impossibility—of having any assurance in advance that the outcome of a militarily enforced overturn of the existing regime, particularly in South Africa, after what might very well be a bitter war of attrition, would not turn out to be worse, or at least as unacceptable, as what now exists.

It is difficult to imagine that the logic of history will not be that the overwhelming majorities of the blacks in Southern Africa will somehow, in ways which still remain hidden from them as well as from us, take over from the whites; perhaps at first sharing control and then achieving the kind of majority rule accepted in much of the rest of the world. Or it may be that the overturn will take a far more cataclysmic form.

The outstanding Negro leader, DuBois, in 1900 uttered a prophecy which has since been repeated many times. He said the problem of the twentieth century is the problem of color—the relation of the darker to the lighter races of men in Asia and Africa, in America and in the islands of the sea. Now, as in 1900, it remains the problem of the twentieth century, and it may be the problem of the twenty-first century as well.

## NOTES

1. George Shepperson, "Notes on Negro American Influences on the Emergence of African Nationalism" in William John Hanna, ed., *Independent Black Africa* (Chicago: 1964), pp. 195–197.

2. Among many other sources, see Ernest Dunbar, *The Black Expatriates* (New York: 1968) for the detailed personal stories of a number of Negro Americans who have settled abroad, some of them in Africa.

# 9

# Southern Africa and United States Policy: A Consideration of Alternatives

*John Marcum*

The great significance of southern Africa for Americans lies in the fact that it involves issues of racial, economic, and political injustice so stark and so closely related to our own society's greatest shortcomings that the failure of Americans to respond adequately raises doubts about the sincerity of our avowed human commitments at home as well as abroad. Like unimplemented domestic ideals, annual American preachments against South African apartheid and Portuguese colonialism at the United Nations must also prompt skepticism about American motives so long as this country continues to help support these same systems that it denounces.

The credibility of American efforts to overcome color prejudice and to create a more equitable society at home is, in particular, vitiated by the conscious or subconscious injection of a racial double standard into foreign policy. When the United States applies different sets of standards to its relationships

This chapter is a revised and lengthened version of an article that appeared in *Africa Today*, 14, No. 5 (October 1967): 5–13. Copyright held by *Africa Today*, Denver, Colo.

with Europe and Africa, this is viewed by many as not just a recognition of very real discrepancies in power but as a true measure of American attitudes toward the vast, colored, nonwhite majority of mankind. During the Stalinist era, when political liberty in Western Europe was threatened from within and without, the United States responded with decisiveness, with a Marshall Plan, a Truman Doctrine, and an Atlantic defense system. But there is no Radio Free South Africa. The enclave of Lesotho scarcely assumes for America the symbolic importance of a beleaguered West Berlin. The United States has not related to the "race curtain" of South Africa as it did to the "iron curtain" of Europe.

Some Americans moralize about Southern Africa. Because it is anticommunist, however, most accept the embrace of its rulers, self-proclaimed defenders of a racially and politically deformed version of Western culture. Most importantly, in relating to Southern Africa, Americans fail to assert the unwarped, liberating values in Western culture. They fail to do so because, perhaps somewhat absent-mindedly, they have come to possess a vested interest in ideals and institutions that totally contradict their own stated national purpose. Such a policy of complicity could lead to tragic consequences on the magnitude of another Vietnam.

What are the internal dynamics and external ramifications of the Southern African situation? What is current American policy and involvement? What policy alternatives are open to the United States?

## The Internal Dynamics of Southern Africa

Within the white redoubt of Afrikanerdom, the rule of the Nationalist party led by Prime Minister J. B. Vorster has never been stronger as measured in electoral victories, economic prosperity, and the silence of the African. The only possible

short-run threat to its continued hegemony lies in the bid for
political power being made by a new, even more extreme
Afrikaner group, the Herstigte Nationale party. Within the
dominant European racial caste of 3.5 million, first the Liberals
and then the Progressives faded as a serious challenge to the
system of white supremacy. The United Party gradually became more royal than the king and lately has come to criticize
the government for being too generous in its conceptions of
home rule for the Transkei and other African reserves, or
Bantustans. Prospects for peaceful change through the liberaliza-
tion of white attitudes have never been more bleak.

The nearly two million Afrikaans-speaking South African
Coloureds have been told that they may not even share that
13 percent of the country to be set aside for Bantustans.
Because of their color, they shall have neither vote nor homeland—just an impotent, government "packed" advisory council
and perpetual dependency on the white for the modest privileges
of their caste. A similarly voteless limbo has been reserved for
the country's 600,000 Indians.

The country's 13,000,000 Africans are permitted to earn a bit
more and to consume a bit more as time goes by. As of 1965,
however, an African gold miner earned between $15 and $50
a month while his white counterpart earned between $319 and
$420.[1] And during the period from March 1962 to March 1967,
although African industrial wages rose by 33 percent, white
wages went up by 43 percent. Moreover, in general white wages
are growing faster than black wages so that the gulf between
them is widening.[2] The government has disallowed moves to up-
grade skills and positions open to Africans, has instead encouraged the development of automation in order to minimize
European reliance upon highly trained, and thus potentially
dangerous, Africans, has banned all African nationalist parties
and has jailed thousands of those who have attempted to defy the
system. Even a study group of the Dutch Reformed Church

reported in 1965 that the practice of recruiting a huge migrant work force to man the mines and factories of urban areas constitutes a "cancer that festers in the life of the African." [3] Separated from his family, segregated from social contact with other racial castes, and subject to being "endorsed out" or back to the rural poverty of his homeland reserve at the government's pleasure, the African becomes an uprooted, propertyless refugee in his own country.

Alienated, rebellious, often nihilistic, with no legal channels for protest, the more than 4 million urban Africans can only turn upon themselves in destructive frustration. The broken families, sexual promiscuity, alcoholism, high crime rates—the phenomenon of the *tsotsi*,[4] in other words, the antisocial or escapist behavior found within urban African society, dulls the spear of the African's resistance to white domination. In turn, the white ruling stratum of society is able to find comfort and justification for its rule from the social havoc it has wrought. It may hope to prolong its domination by means of a system that destroys self-respect, indoctrinates young minds with belief in their own inferiority, and stresses divisive tribal loyalties and parochial languages in segregated schools. Through a process that might be qualified as psychic genocide,[5] the capacity of the non-European effectively to challenge those who rule over him is destroyed. This is the most frightening, if not demonic, aspect of the apartheid system, namely the degree to which it may be self-perpetuating.

The Afrikaner church study group cited earlier has prophesied: "The laws of God have ordained that the whites shall not remain untouched by the diseases that are destroying the moral life of the Bantu." [6] And certainly the longer the delusions of racial supremacy and the repression of police-state rule curse the peoples of South Africa—whether African, Indian, Coloured or White—the more warped the society becomes. If present trends are not altered by external pressure, the ultimate reckoning in human hatred, violence, suffering and self-destruction may be so great as to lead only and inevitably to new, intensified forms of tyranny—unless, of course, someone dispatches an army of social psychiatrists.

The situation in the Portuguese territories of Angola and Mozambique is different but not much more promising. With their right to self-determination assertedly used up during the process and aftermath of Portuguese conquest, the 12 million persons of these two countries are defined by Lisbon as simply black Portuguese who happen to live in Africa. Though less than 5 percent can read or write Portuguese, and though none have the freedom to express dissenting opinions about their identity, Lisbon confidently insists that they have been assimilated for all time within the mystic body of a multicontinental Portuguese nation. Unlike the South African government, however, the Lusitanian regime has not been able to suppress all organized African resistance. Limited but sustained insurgency ties down an expeditionary force of 130,000 men, the bulk of Portugal's army, while the preindustrial economy of Portugal is drained of $400 million annually for military and security operations.

Nevertheless, the post-Salazar government of Prime Minister Marcello Caetano refuses to budge from the dogma that Angola and Mozambique *are* Portugal. Coffee, diamonds, and most recently, iron and petroleum resources have hiked the real estate value of Angola enormously. The Portuguese administration has belatedly coupled with its military effort a modest program of educational and economic development, launched in order to try to make a reality out of the theory of assimilation. Ironically, though short-run hopes for political change depend upon the progressive escalation of African guerrilla action or a progressive devolution of autonomy upon local (nominally multiracial but predominantly European) territorial governments, long-run promise may be found in the very educational program that is designed to make Africans into Portuguese. In all likelihood the program will render them better able to question, reason, and rebel. On the other hand, however rapidly expanded, Portugal's antiquated and elitist system of education is unlikely to serve adequately the need for a peaceful social, economic, and political revolution that alone might avert the eventuality of a generalized colonial upheaval. And the longer the Portuguese rule by means of their army, police (DGS), and police informers, and by the manipulation of divisive regional and tribal differences, and the longer they fail to introduce that which they deny to themselves, *i.e.,* the institutions and processes of democratic government, the more likely it becomes that the eventual collapse of their authority will leave chaos in its wake.

With UDI, Southern Rhodesia's Unilateral Declaration of Independence, in 1965, the ambiguous situation within that country was brutally clarified. A well-armed minority of less than a quarter of a million Europeans assumed hierarchical rule over some 4 million hapless, politically unorganized Africans, in defiance of the British Crown. Despite promises by exiled African nationalists that there would be a "blood bath" in the event of such a white power grab, UDI did not spark massive unrest, significant sabotage, or sustained guerrilla insurgency. Thanks to arms, will, and bluff, the Rhodesian Front government of Ian Smith was therefore able to cling to political power in spite of economic sanctions sponsored by the British and organized through the United Nations. Also crucial, Pretoria and Lisbon defied those sanctions with impunity. As racial allies they not only continued to provide a trade outlet for Rhodesian goods but also offered material and moral assistance to the rebel regime, while incurring little more than expressions of displeasure on the part of a British government that was unprepared to intervene militarily in defense of its sovereignty. Then, as the inefficacy of a hastily

contrived, gradually applied program of economic sanctions
became increasingly apparent, Prime Minister Harold Wilson
turned not to more forceful action but rather to "talks about
talks" with Ian Smith. London appeared desperate to make any
"honorable" retreat from a showdown that would not wreck
the Commonwealth; but Rhodesia chose to consecrate its victory in a republican constitution that obliged the British to
persevere with a self-denying, ineffective "no trade" policy.
Rhodesia was secured for protracted white rule. Only later, if
African nationalists can overcome factional quarrels and organize a disciplined political underground, can one anticipate
political change. However, this will probably be at the cost
of a bloody racial conflagration.

### The External Ramifications of the Southern African Situation

A few short years ago many observers assumed that the
onrush of African nationalism, which gained momentum in
the late 1950s, would rapidly carry the process or "wind" of
political change all the way to the Cape of Good Hope. Such
prognoses underestimated the resilience of European rule south
of the African Mason and Dixon Line. Hopes of delivery
from the north gradually faded into disillusionment and pes-
simism.

In 1964–65, white South African mercenaries insinuated the
South African issue into the Congo where they saved the government of the former Katanga secessionist, Moise Tshombe,
and defeated militant, avowedly Pan-Africanist rebels in military
operations that carried the representatives of apartheid to the
borders of Uganda and the Sudan. Recalling the days of the
Japanese empire, Pretoria announced its willingness to extend an
economic "co-prosperity sphere" of its own design to the microstates of Lesotho, Botswana, and Swaziland, and to Rhodesia,
the Portuguese colonies, Malawi and beyond. For its part,

meanwhile, the Portuguese government defied the rhetorical wrath of African diplomats within the United Nations and the Organization of African Unity and belligerently countered with threats of military action against Tanzania which it described as a "communist base" from which Mozambican terrorists were attempting to destroy the peace of Portuguese East Africa. Salisbury's UDI produced verbal crusades and divisive debate among frustrated African diplomats following which an embarrassingly small number of states severed diplomatic relations with Great Britain; Zambia was seized by a major economic crisis; but no Pan-African army came forth to rescue the people of Zimbabwe.

Unable to cope effectively with the crises of the Congo or Rhodesia, humiliated and frustrated by the victories of the Moise Tshombes, Ian Smiths, white mercenaries, anti-Castro Cuban pilots, Belgian paratroops, and American planes, the African states flayed out with forensic ire against Western neo-colonialist and CIA plots—then turned upon themselves in mutual recrimination. Differences that had earlier polarized Africa into the more assertedly Pan-African Casablanca bloc and a more introspectively status quo Monrovia bloc resurfaced. Then as a sequence of military coups and civil wars rocked Nigeria, the Sudan, and much of the rest of the continent, as they revealed the fragility of Africa's new states and removed such charismatic Pan-African crusaders as Presidents Ahmed Ben Bella, Kwame Nkrumah, and Modibo Keita from power, it was less the polarization than the introspection that stood out. The self-righteous enthusiasm with which the American press greeted the fall of Kwame Nkrumah only increased the temptation to attribute all these ills and setbacks to the machinations of outsiders in London and Washington who were determined to preserve material interests in Southern Africa. One result was a further alienation of profoundly discouraged and embittered liberation movements from anything Western.

As for these action-oriented southern movements—their forces idled in military and refugee camps in Tanzania, far from the Limpopo—they issued mimeographed tracts in Zambia on the wrong side of the Zambezi or skirmished indecisively though persistently with Portuguese counterinsurgency forces in the thinly populated northern and eastern sectors of Angola and northern regions of Mozambique. Frustrated, like the independent states, they also turned upon themselves, quarreled, fragmented, and blamed their difficulties on the plots of "imperialists and their agents."

By 1967–1969, African liberation movements had made some headway in overcoming the perceptual, behavioral, and technical problems of their exile condition.[7] For example, in August 1967 the African National Congress (ANC) of South Africa and the Zimbabwe African People's Union (ZAPU) launched a joint military operation into Rhodesia. As of 1969 guerrilla action in Angola extended from a nationalist-held "rotten triangle" in the north [8] to the vast, lightly peopled savanna of the east and south,[9] though the effectiveness of guerrilla action was undermined by the division of Angolan nationalists into three competing movements.[10] Elsewhere, the Mozambique Liberation Front (FRELIMO) had solidly implanted itself south of the Ruvuma River and was attempting to move southward toward the economic and demographic centers of the colony.[11] And there were even some sporadic guerrilla sorties into the Caprivi-Ovamboland areas of South-West Africa by members of the South-West Africa People's Organization (SWAPO).

By and large, however, African insurgency had not yet developed to the point where it was seriously affecting the racial and political order within Southern Africa, an order which showed no signs of improving. Nine years after the outbreak of fighting in Angola's northern coffee country, a small-scale insurgency continued; but meanwhile coffee production had grown from 168.6 thousand metric tons in 1961 to 217.8 thousand metric tons in 1966 and was still rising.[12] The hold of some 4 million Europeans over more than 30 million non-Europeans (1:8 ratio) tightened. Furthermore, the counterthrust of white power produced a destructive backlash of racial bitterness, cynicism, and frustration among thousands of politically aware and concerned persons in independent African states who view South African apartheid as the anti-Christ symbol of the African Revolution.

Surely, however, if ever the "objective conditions" for an eventual revolution, a proper Marxist-Leninist revolution, were being systematically created, and if ever the role of the United States was lending itself to the most unflattering interpretations of Chinese and Swedish, Marxist and Christian, New Left and Quaker critics, it was in Southern Africa. In giving moral and material support to the African cause, both Peking and Moscow were displaying a superior ability to act upon the basis of historical perspective and self-interest, let alone moral principle.

### American Policy and Involvement

American policy toward Southern Africa may be described as a contradictory tandem of lamentation and laissez-faire. The American government proclaims support for the principle of self-determination, including the right of Africans to govern themselves through institutions of their own choice. It laments apartheid as a denial of the principle of government by the consent of the governed. It laments the refusal of Portugal to admit the principle of self-determination for the same reason. And it laments a Rhodesian independence that excludes the African majority from an equitable participation in the government.

With regard to the Portuguese colonies, former Assistant Secretary of State for African Affairs G. Mennen Williams has described American policy as seeking "to impose no special formula" but as contemplating "an immediate recognition of the people's timely right to choose independence or other forms of association or disassociation" and as recognizing the necessity of "steps being taken to prepare the people for self-government as rapidly as possible." [13]

Concerning South Africa, Williams has said that American policy recognized the necessity of convincing the government of that country that apartheid contains "the seeds of destruction for South Africa, as well as trouble for the rest of the world." Acting upon these assumptions, then, the American government is said by Williams to have sought over time to persuade Lisbon and Pretoria "by every diplomatic means" to engage in a "dialogue" with the Africans concerned.[14]

What has been the result of American importuning? Diplomatic pressure has proven ineffectual. American advice has been completely ignored. Nevertheless, American policy-makers have themselves chosen to ignore this failure. Within the forum of the United Nations, the United States regularly declares its abhorrence of apartheid and colonialism but then justifies inaction by asserting that these blights constitute no threat to the peace. The Nixon Administration has carried on the tradition,[15] although in his address before the United Nations General Assembly in September 1969, entitled "Strengthening the Total Fabric of Peace," President Richard Nixon did not once mention Africa, let alone South Africa.[16]

American officials express earnest hope that conditions will improve while almost all indicators point to further deterioration. State Department spokesmen argue against a cessation of American investment because it "could seriously handicap our ability to carry on a dialogue with South Africa," yet admit that race relations in Southern Africa "have worsened despite the efforts of the outside world whether of persuasion, condemnation, or pressure." [17] Responsible American officials

admit that African nationalists in fact "feel increasingly frustrated in their efforts to achieve political expression," [18] but with
the notable exception of an arms embargo on South Africa
and support for British-United Nations sanctions against
Rhodesia, the American government is content to lament injustice and label as extremist those who advocate that it face
the implications of the failure of moral suasion. Under both
Democratic and Republican administrations, the United States
has doggedly followed policies that have admittedly failed, has
confusedly reacted to events that it might have influenced, and
has rather pathetically explained that it is still seeking ideas,
studying means, or considering initiatives to meet an "intracta-
ble" situation.

The contradictory and self-defeating duality of American
policy becomes clear when the reality of America's military,
economic, and racial involvement in southern Africa is con-
trasted with its invocation of principle. It is the laissez-faire, not
the lamentation (which may, of course, mislead the unwary
about American intentions) that does the principal harm.
Americans permit themselves to enjoy military and economic
privileges, even discriminate against their own citizens, and
otherwise forfeit their independence and integrity in order to
safeguard these privileges.

### Military Involvement

American military involvement in southern Africa comes
primarily through ties to Portugal within the framework of the
North Atlantic Alliance. Portugal was admitted to that alliance
because of the strategic value of the Azores Islands and the
Iberian Peninsula, despite its hostility toward Western democratic values and practices. In April 1963, a ranking official in
the Pentagon described the importance of American base rights
in the Azores this way: "Approximately 75 percent of normal
U.S. military air traffic to Europe and the Middle East transits

the air facilities on Terceira Island, and this base would be indispensable in the event of an emergency requiring U.S. forces to be sent to those areas." [19] Portugal ably capitalized upon this asserted indispensability of the Azores to an Atlantic defense system that permitted Portugal to send the bulk of its armed forces to sub-Equatorial Africa far from the Atlantic defense area. In the words of former White House aide Theodore Sorensen, Lisbon used the Atlantic Islands as a "wedge" and "tried every form of diplomatic blackmail" in order to obtain American approval of Portuguese colonial policy.[20] As a result, the United States refused to support United Nations resolutions that would have imposed economic sanctions on Portugal—sanctions designed to persuade it to implement the principle of self-determination. But American complicity was more than passive. In spite of the absence of any perceptible signs that Portugal might be prepared to alter its policies, the United States continued to provide direct and indirect financial and material assistance that shored up military efforts against African nationalists seeking independence by the only means left open to them, *i.e.*, violent action.

In 1963, the delivery of American T37C pilot trainers helped build up the Portuguese air force at a time when the principal mission of its pilots was to bomb, strafe, and napalm African insurgents. As of 1964, at a time when Portugal maintained some 85,000 of its then estimated total of 115,000 troops in Africa, thousands of miles from the North Atlantic defense zone,[21] the American government was officially scheduled to deliver over $34 million in military aid to Portugal as a contribution to North Atlantic security.[22]

The United States has maintained a ban of disputed effectiveness against the use in Africa of military equipment that it furnishes to Portugal in conjunction with NATO. In 1967, when it renewed the loan of two naval escort destroyers, it did so with the stipulation that they were not to be used south of the Tropic of Cancer. Nevertheless, such continued, if modest, military assistance ($3.2 million in 1968) and financial grants and credits ($6 million in 1968) from the United States obviously releases other matériel and funds for use in Lisbon's colonial wars.[23] These wars are costing Portugal dearly. Roughly 45 percent of its annual budget goes for military expenditures, and such derivative costs as inflation and nonproductive use of scarce capital must weigh heavily upon its future.

During António Salazar's rule, Foreign Minister Alberto Nogueira set out deftly to maximize American entanglement in Portugal's military strategy. Thus in 1965 he cited what he described as the American "doctrine of legitimate retaliation in Vietnam" as a justification for possible Portuguese action against Tanzania, a "dangerous Communist base" for terrorist incursions into Mozambique. By choosing a NATO ministerial meeting as the occasion for his veiled threat to bomb north of the Ruvuma, by drawing parallels with the Vietnamese war in which articulated African sympathies lie overwhelmingly with the Viet Cong, and by defining the threat to Mozambique as Communist, not nationalist, Nogueira deliberately spun a web in which Portuguese and American policy might appear to be identical.[24] He thereby made certain that if his country should ever make good on its threat, all Africa would assume that it was with American approval. Washington never publicly disassociated itself from such embraces.

President John Kennedy sent a military man, Admiral George Anderson, as his ambassador to Portugal. After making a well-publicized trip to Angola and Mozambique in March 1964, the admiral was quoted as saying that he had been "tremendously impressed" with the progress and well-being that he found in those territories. Such statements, of course, served further to identify the United States with Portugal's military endeavors. All this infuriated African nationalist leaders. The late Dr. Eduardo Mondlane, president of FRELIMO, con-

cluded that such testimony as Anderson's constituted evidence
that "the United States of America cannot identify itself with
our ideals for self-determination and independence." Noting
that the American admiral's visit was followed shortly thereafter by the visit of a ranking South African general, Dr.
Mondlane said he expected that the United States "like the
Republic of South Africa, will intervene against us in the
forthcoming armed conflict with Portugal." [25]

In late 1969, at the invitation of the United States Army, a
Portuguese military mission comprising directors of the Practical Schools of Infantry, Military Engineering, Artillery and
Cavalry visited military schools and establishments in the
United States.[26] It seemed unlikely that Washington could ask
these visitors to refrain from using anything learned during
this mission when training Portuguese soldiers destined for
service in Africa, *i.e.,* most of their trainees.

Outside of a National Aeronautics and Space Administration
(NASA) tracking station, occasional naval use of refueling
services, and a heightened respect for the strategic importance
of the Cape following the closing of the Suez Canal, American
relationships with South Africa have contrastingly little military
significance. Indeed, the United States has respected a United
Nations embargo on arms sales to South Africa, causing
Pretoria to turn to such a *franc tireur* as Gaullist France to
obtain helicopters, jet aircraft, submarines, and other war
materiél.

### Economic Involvement

America's principal entanglement with "the republic" is
economic. Over 275 American firms have holdings or do business there, and American investors earn over $100 million
annually. The United States has a favorable balance of trade
with South Africa: in 1968 exports totalled $455 million and
imports $253 million.[27] Over half of the American exports to

South Africa consist of capital goods which further industrial growth. Total American investment amounts to approximately $800 million and pays returns of upwards of 17 percent per year. American bank loans helped South Africa out of the economic crisis that left it vulnerable to international pressures in 1960–1961 pursuant to African nationalist unrest and the Sharpeville massacre. By 1963 American investment had risen to the rate of $35 million annually and by 1966 it was 45 percent above what it had been before Sharpeville.[28]

The full significance of the laissez-faire policy that has left Americans free to invest in South Africa's quick-profit, cheap-labor economy can be easily missed. One may point to the United Kingdom's much deeper and less soluble involvement with its South African investments of more than $3 billion. And one may note that the South African economy is now self-propelling and no longer dependent upon outside investment. Beyond the fact that any trade and investment strengthens the system, however, two aspects of American involvement must be underscored. First, American capital, managerial skills, and technical know-now have been and are contributing to those sectors of the South African economy that further the advantages of European over African and produce self-sufficiency and thus immunity from pressure by international sanctions. Developing highly automated industries that require skills reserved for Europeans helps to reduce the relative importance of unskilled African labor. Ford, Chrysler, and General Motors, in striving to produce "all South African" cars, further the invulnerability of South Africa to the threat of economic sanctions. Moreover, as *The South African Financial Gazette* has observed, "in times of emergency, or war" such automotive plants "could be turned over rapidly to the production of weapons and other strategic requirements for the defense of Southern Africa."[29]

A second aspect of American economic involvement that

deserves special note is the extent to which it permits particular interests to define America's national interests. Take just one example from among many. Milton P. Higgins, chairman of the International Norton Company of the United States, spoke in January 1965, at ceremonies opening an extension to his abrasives company's South African subsidiary, ceremonies graced by the presence of the acting American consul-general in Johannesburg. The South African press quoted Higgins as saying: "There are those people in the United States who believe this country will blow up within a few years. But I don't believe that, otherwise we would not invest in South Africa. I think this is going to remain a strong country, led by White people. I think you are going to remain in control. I think foreign countries should leave the politics of South Africa alone. It they leave you alone you will get on and do a great job." [30] In 1969, a survey of American and Canadian business executives working in South Africa revealed a strong pro-South African sentiment: 92 percent of those polled foresaw no serious racial or economic unrest and 81 percent approved of South Africa's racial segregation as "at least an attempt to develop a solution." Those polled were part of a community of an estimated 6,000 white North Americans who are associated with the local operations of large American corporations.[31] To argue as some do that by helping to create an economy of affluence such American corporations may help to persuade the white community of South Africa increasingly to permit nonwhites to participate and share power within their society is to engage in wishful, often self-serving speculation. Analyses of the impact of industrialization upon South Africa provide no evidence so far of a modifying or moderating influence on racial attitudes.[32]

In contrast to its economic position in South Africa, the United States had very little economic interest in Portuguese Africa before 1965. There was an important exception to this.

The United States was already the largest buyer of Angolan robusta coffee, around $55 million yearly. But it was only with Portugal's enactment of new "open door" foreign investment laws in 1964 that American and other Western capital began to take an intense interest. Indeed, *The New York Times* predicted that the broadened guarantees and simplified procedures offered foreign firms might lead to "a surge of new investments" from America, Britain, West Germany, and South Africa.[33] And in the absence of any government initiatives to insure that American private interests would not confound American national interests with the destiny of Portuguese colonialism, *The New York Times'* prediction proved prophetic.

American and other foreign capital began pouring into Angola and Mozambique. Gulf Oil invested some $150 million to develop a dramatically rich oil field in Cabinda. As of 1969, other American companies had acquired diamond concessions, were preparing to exploit sulphur and phosphate deposits, and were otherwise preparing to participate in Angola's incipient economic boom. American oil companies were also prospecting a promising stretch of the Mozambican coast, and American trade with the two colonies soared. In 1968, it reached just under $100 million in imports and to $52 million in exports from the United States.[34]

Portuguese efforts to obtain American corporate involvement in the immense Cabora Bassa hydroelectric project (a $493 million project with a final generating capacity of 4,000 megawatts, almost twice that of Aswan) in Mozambique failed. But a bizarre and improbable American press item of September 1969 suggested that Portugal was prepared to go to some lengths to share African wealth with Americans. According to the *San Francisco Chronicle*, a group of persons headed by Frank Ricciardi, board chairman of Richton International, managed to purchase (or just obtain use of?) about 6 million acres (some 9,370 square miles) of Mozambique for a "private

club for wild game enthusiasts like himself and Prentiss Cobb
Hale of San Francisco." [35] Whatever the specifics of the arrangement, the symbolism was powerful.

American participation in the United Nations program of
economic sanctions against Rhodesia at least initially curtailed
American economic support for Southern Africa's newest and
least secure white regime. Yet by mid-1969, Southern congress-
men and right-wing lobbyists in Washington who sympathized
with the white-supremacist government of Ian Smith, along
with American corporations with Rhodesian investments, were
pressuring President Richard Nixon to keep the American
consulate in Salisbury open (contrary to expressed British de-
sires). Union Carbide and Foote Mineral, which own Rhodesian chrome mines, were "among the interested parties"
applying pressure.[36]

### Racial Involvement

Afro-Americans figure prominently in the American foreign
service throughout Africa. Yet none may serve in the various
services of the largest American mission in Africa. American
foreign service personnel policy for South Africa is in this
sense set by Pretoria and not Washington. The gentleman's
agreement not to mention this was broken in July 1965 when
Prime Minister Verwoerd threw caution to the wind at a
political rally and announced that his government would never
accept the assignment of an Afro-American to NASA's South
African tracking station. Some days earlier his government had
already created a racial incident by gratuitously announcing
that no mixed air crews might land planes from the passing
American aircraft carrier *Independence,* thereby causing the
ship to be refueled at sea. For a moment it appeared that
because of these incidents the American government might
take a stand against policies that forced it to discriminate
against its own citizens. But on July 3, *The New York Times*

reported that apparently "a decision has been taken on both sides to look the other way and avoid an embarrassing confrontation." The report said that the American embassy had refused all comment on the racial affronts and had seemingly refrained from pressing for any clarification. Once again, on the crucial issue of race, American action belied professed values.

In the absence of any organized protest by the American Negro Leadership Conference on Africa or other civil-rights groups, the issue remained unjoined. More recently, militant groups such as CORE, the Black Panthers, and other black organizations have added the cause of Southern Africa to their own . . . at least emotionally. After all, the common culture of segregated urban poverty forms a natural bond between many Afro-Americans and Southern Africans. And there were signs, such as the new militancy of black academics within the African Studies Association, that black Americans will be making insistent demands for a greater say in the formation of American foreign policy toward Africa.[37] Yet until this demand becomes an integral part of the platform of a well-organized and powerful black American political movement, white, and only white, American businessmen, technicians, and diplomats are likely to continue to enjoy the comforts and cheap domestic service of South African suburbia. And in the United States, white and black Americans who own stock in or are employed by firms investing in and trading with South Africa will remain the automatic beneficiaries of an economic system built upon racial exploitation.

The American government has even absent-mindedly reinforced white supremacy in South Africa by giving substantial financial assistance to a collective Western program of organized migration to the Republic. Between 1952 and 1965, the Intergovernmental Committee for European Migration (ICEM) brought over 25,000 Europeans to South Africa—

some 4,300 of whom arrived in 1965 alone. Most of this emigration was made up of much-needed skilled workers and their families. Such immigrants help to offset economic pressures for lowering the job color bar and for training Africans in modern skills. The American government contributed $4.9 million or 29.77 percent of the ICEM administrative budget for the fiscal year 1965 and thereby helped to swell the ranks of apartheid's ruling racial caste.[38] When questioned about this, State Department officials maintained that because ICEM assistance to South Africa constituted but a fraction of its activities, such assistance did not warrant an official protest or cut in the American subsidy.

### American Alternatives

Aside from dropping the lament and transforming the laissez-faire into a forthright support for the economic and political status quo in Southern Africa, what are the alternatives open to American policy-makers? If one assumes that the objective of American policy should be to promote, or at least not to work against, racial justice and political self-determination (an assumption not likely to be shared by some relevant and influential senators like Strom Thurmond and even William Fulbright), how should this objective be pursued?

Few, if any, would argue for a unilateral American intervention to impose "just standards or solutions." The fiascoes of the Cuban, Dominican, and Vietnamese interventions counsel too strongly against the efficacy and morality of such ventures. And before supporting a collective intervention under the United Nations, it would seem only reasonable that Americans should first take action to see to it that they have related honestly to the issue presented, that they have exhausted all other available means to a solution.

To do so would demand a prescience and sense of national purpose a notch above the standard conduct of American foreign relations. And yet the hard-core problems of Southern Africa require that the United States transcend the constraints of alliances, racial prejudice, and economic profit and that it act with the sense of independence and purposefulness that governed its policy on Suez in 1956 and Katanga in 1960–61. The issues at stake call for a firm policy of disengagement and affirmation. Accordingly, the United States should disengage from support and identification with the status quo and should affirm its support for change by taking concrete and constructive action.

Such a policy of disentanglement designed to restore American freedom of action should replace the laissez-faire of current policy with ground rules to govern military, economic, and racial relationships with Southern Africa. The United States applied such a consistent set of rules to its relations with Stalinist Russia. Thus in keeping with American national interest and purpose, policy guidelines should firmly, if selectively, disassociate the United States from the support of that which it condemns.

The time is long since past when the inequities of an unregulated, laissez-faire economy could be politically tolerated within American society. Given the absence of either effective international constraints or self-imposed national restraints, however, economic power functions irresponsibly at the interstate level. Americans by and large see no inconsistency in arguing that if what is good for General Motors is not necessarily good for America, it is nevertheless unquestionably good for South Africa or Angola. The issue obviously goes well beyond American relations with Southern Africa. The disaster of a laissez-faire policy that assumes no responsibility for the consequences of admittedly self-interested private economic power operating in weak and vulnerable preindustrial countries (or in countries under caste rule based on racial ascription) is patent—yet disallowed.

Disallowed or not, the logic that suggests that American economic, military, and racial relationships abroad (private or public) should not be permitted to operate at cross purposes with stated American diplomatic or political objectives seems overwhelming. Just how general ground rules covering such relationships might be applied in the case of southern Africa may be seen best by examining separately relationships with the particular countries involved.

### Angola and Mozambique

American military and economic relationships with Portugal weigh against the African nationalist cause in Angola, Mozambique, and the embattled West African colony of Guinea-Bissau. Disengagement from further support of Portugal's military campaigns against insurgent nationalists would suggest several initiatives.

First, the American government could act to reduce its dependence upon Portugal, meaning upon the Azores bases. Recent technological advance, e.g., long-range aircraft, has in fact reduced the importance of these installations. The Defense Department, of course, is not concerned with the need to escape Portuguese diplomatic "blackmail." In the words of James Reston, "Washington needed the Azores as a ferry base in the [Second World War] for aircraft of limited range; it needs the Azores no longer, but the old arrangements go on." [39] Required, then, is a political decision to evacuate these bases.[40]

Second, given both the redundancy of the Azores and a growing politico-military detente in Europe, the American government could begin to formulate its policies toward the problems posed by Portuguese colonial rule in Africa in terms of its own, as distinct from Lisbon's, perceptions and priorities.[41]

From such a vantage point it might then come to appear self-evident that inasmuch as Portugal's armed forces are bogged down in an ultimately vain effort to suppress African nationalism in colonies far removed from the North Atlantic area, the United States would be justified in cutting off all military assistance and imposing an embargo on all arms sales to Portugal. Another NATO ally, Norway, did this long ago.

Third, the United States still has time to blow the whistle on the investment of American capital and technology in Angola and Mozambique before it results in an entanglement comparable to that reached in South Africa. Granted South Africa, France, and West Germany, who have already eclipsed the United States as military providers, would then preempt the economic field. But at least American integrity would be restored. Furthermore, the United States would not suffer in the slightest if it should cease purchasing Angolan coffee, a plentiful commodity on the world market, or should initiate proceedings to exclude Portugal from the International Coffee Agreement.

Conceivably, even the prospect of such American military and economic disengagement might jar Lisbon into a reconsideration of its uncompromising stand against African self-determination. Moreover, a quiet parallel offer to help a more Europe-oriented Caetano government to modernize metropolitan Portugal (where illiteracy is still around 40 percent and from where some 80,000 underprivileged emigrate annually) might further encourage such a reconsideration.

In any event, a disengagement policy ought to be accompanied by an affirmative, compensatory prod toward reform. It should also include a sober government pledge to restrain private American corporations or educational-cultural institutions from attempting to rush in and supersede Portugal with a new "private" American hegemony. Such assurances of self-restraint (ground rules) could set an exemplary precedent.

*South Africa*

Disengagement from South Africa would be more difficult. In addition, it would be even less likely to achieve much more than a freeing of American policy (but not Africans) from the shackles of racial bias.

To expect American business firms voluntarily to abandon the high profits of the South African economy to foreign competitors because of moral principle is, of course, to expect the improbable. Again the government would need to provide ground rules. There are several alternatives open to it. It could declare further investment and bank loans to be against American national interest and purpose and also promote the liquidation of investments already made. It could levy a selective antiapartheid (or disincentive) tax on profits and income made in and on trading done with South Africa. The proceeds from such a tax might then be invested in the enclave territories of Lesotho, Botswana, and Swaziland. The government could also apply pressure on American businesses to offer wages, training, health facilities, and even educational opportunities to African employees in such a combination as to compensate for (and thus reduce) what can only be described as excess profits earned at African expense.

Application of the principle of disengagement earlier would have ruled out a host of needless supportive entanglements. Take a few examples:

1. The United States Bureau of Reclamation would not have signed a $6.3 million contract with an international civil engineering consortium, in which South African companies predominated, to build a five-mile tunnel through the San Juan Mountains of Colorado.[42]

2. At a time when automation was being viewed as a means for rendering the African redundant and for further reducing his chances to attain economic or political power, the Ameri-

can government would not have programmed the South African
minister of transportation, Mr. J. B. Shoeman, on a study
tour of automation in the United States designed to help his
government automate the railroads and airports of South
Africa.[43]

3. Given widespread African fears and international speculation that uranium-rich South Africa may try to develop both
nuclear energy and nuclear weapons, the American Atomic
Energy Commission would not have trained South African
technicians at the Oak Ridge National Laboratory in Ten-
nessee. Also, it would not have loaned the reactor consultant
to whom the South Africans consider themselves "largely
indebted for the successful commission" of their first nuclear
reactor.[44] Subsidizing South Africa with a share of the American sugar import quota and authorizing South African Air-
ways to fly the New York-Johannesburg route in planes that
necessarily exclude nonwhite Americans constitute two current examples of how the United States is still unnecessarily
accommodating racial inequity.

Related to the need for economic disengagement is a parallel
need for a restructuring of cultural and scientific relations with
South Africa. The guiding principle should be that of a strict
*quid pro quo* and mutuality of benefits. At the present time
the relationship is most unequal. Considerable numbers of white
South African students are increasing the technological and
scientific advantage of European over African by studying in
such American institutions as the Massachusetts Institute of
Technology, while the Case Institute of Technology (Cleveland) has helped to build and operate a nuclear physics laboratory in neutrino research at Bokesburg in the Transvaal. On
the other hand, the South African government has refused
passports to Africans seeking to come to this country. For
example, it rejected such requests from the chairman of the

opposition Democratic party, Knowledge Guzana, in the sup-
posedly self-governing Transkei, and from a prominent Zulu
chief, Gatsha Buthelezi, both of whom had been awarded
foreign leadership grants to visit the United States as guests of
the American government. As for the reverse flow, South African authorities deny visas to a growing list of American scholars
and newsmen and bar visits by Afro-Americans of all professions. Arthur Ashe is not even allowed in to play tennis.

A proper balance should be restored to this lopsided situation. The United States can insist that Africans from South
Africa be granted passports to enable them to pursue scientific
and technological studies in this country, barring which visas
will not be given to white South African students. The United
States can insist upon reciprocity and retaliate suitably when
its scholars, journalists, missionaries, or athletes are denied
visas or are encumbered by travel restrictions. The American
government can reasonably demand that South Africa—and
Portugal—grant all American citizens visitor and transit visas
on the basis of the same generous standards that it applies to
South Africans and Portuguese. If the demand for reciprocity
is denied then American practice can be adjusted accordingly.
At the same time, both American governmental and private
exchange programs with South Africa might well be overhauled
and placed upon a basis of strict reciprocity that neither dis-
advantages Africans nor discriminates against Afro-Americans.[45]

Economic disengagement should also release American
diplomacy from the chore of dissimulating disagreements over
basic human rights in order to protect economic interests. When
William M. Rountree assumed the post of American ambassador to South Africa in late 1965, he was quoted by the South
African press as having defined his "main objective" as that
of "improved relations" between two countries which he emphasized had long been in "close association." [46] So as not to

justify charges of self-interested hypocrisy, American diplomats might better speak out publicly, politely, and unequivocally on the basic issues which separate the two countries. Moreover, basic changes are called for in the comportment and make-up of the American diplomatic mission in South Africa. Political ground rules are needed so that Americans no longer ask others to give up privileges that they do not deny themselves.

First, it is only equitable that white Americans accept the onus of insisting that Afro-Americans be permitted to serve within South Africa in numbers proportionate to and in a style in keeping with their service in American missions elsewhere in Africa. They should have to be granted the same professional and social courtesies granted to white Americans—or to diplomats from Malawi. Second, political integrity would suggest that all American government personnel and their families be instructed to attend no segregated social functions, golf clubs, restaurants, schools, etc., to do without the luxury of cheap African domestics, and to refrain from any statements or actions that could imply approval of the policies that the American government repudiates in the halls of the United Nations. Should Pretoria react negatively to such measures designed to restore honor to the official American presence in South Africa, the United States should be prepared to suffer the consequences. South Africa might have to be reclassified as a hardship post to be manned by fewer persons who reflect a policy that attaches more value to convictions than to comfortable living.

## South-West Africa and Rhodesia

In the cases of these two countries there are clear legal bases for international intervention against illegal governments. In 1966, an anticlimactic decision of the International Court of Justice not to decide whether apartheid legally annulled South Africa's mandate over South-West Africa nevertheless left intact the possibility of political action by the United Nations. Accordingly, the General Assembly "terminated" the mandate because of South Africa's refusal to abide by the mandate's terms and decided to place the territory under direct United Nations administration. Predictably, South Africa refused to give up its power over the territory. In 1969, the United States supported a followup resolution of the Security Council that called upon South Africa "to immediately withdraw its administration from the territory." In the face of the certitude of continued South African defiance, however, Washington supported the resolution because "it wisely [did] not commit the Council to the narrow path of mandatory sanctions." [47] To continue in this fashion to support United Nations resolutions that call for compliant action, to condemn defiance of these resolutions by South Africa and, just as inconsistently, to continue to oppose sanctions designed to implement these same resolutions is to invite cynicism and ridicule. Such a policy risks irreparable damage to the United Nations.

In the case of Rhodesia the legal authority of both the British Crown and the United Nations has been defied. Economic sanctions are in force—but are failing because of the noncompliance of two members of the United Nations, Portugal and, once again, South Africa. The present Assistant Secretary of State for African Affairs David D. Newsom has said that due to this defiance, "An early solution to the problem does not seem in sight. Nevertheless, we feel that our obligations to the Charter of the United Nations and our position as a leader of the free world justify our present policy." [48] But can the pursuit of a policy that one knows is failing be considered intelligent or moral? Does it make any sense to continue to pretend that a program of sanctions constitutes an adequate response when Rhodesia's economy is not only surviving but growing, especially in its industrial sector? It makes no more sense than to pretend that voting to change the name of

South-West Africa to Namibia represents "progress." So long as the United States opposes the extension of United Nations sanctions to meet Portuguese and South African defiance of the world organization, there will be no significant change, unless by guerrilla action, in either South West Africa or Rhodesia. All of which brings the discussion back to the necessity for action to disentangle the United States from its supportive relationships with Portugal and South Africa.

## In Conclusion

What might properly follow a policy of selective disengagment would depend in some measure upon just how such a policy affected the chemistry of the Southern African cauldron. Some of the possibilities for creative action, other than those already mentioned, however, can be readily envisioned. In support of nonviolent, long-range change, the United States could offer to develop higher education and technical training programs in Botswana, Lesotho, and Swaziland. Economic assistance to develop the economies of these three states could also help to create healthy alternative models of society that would invite attention and provoke comparisons on the part of Africans and Europeans in the rest of southern Africa. The United States might even establish a powerful radio transmitter to beam educational programming throughout southern Africa in Portuguese, English, and the vernacular languages. Such broadcasts might extend in scope from the primary to the technical and university level, with literature, examinations, and degrees provided through correspondence.

Hopes for change within a reasonably short time span depend upon the fortunes of African liberation movements. Thus, direct financial aid to these movements, if screened through an international agency (United Nations or Organization of African Unity) so as to avoid either the pitfalls of patron-client relations or "king-making" where there are rival movements, might become a real postdisengagement policy-alternative, one that could come to enjoy compelling Afro-American support.

Only a prior or concomitant program of selective disengagement, however, would give the United States any right to embark upon such programs of selective reengagement. As it stands, American policy is alienating Africans and leading to conditions in which American options more and more are being reduced to a choice between two extremes: continue supporting the pro-American Batistas who have jailed, banned, or exterminated all democratic opposition, or try to assuage or disarm the wrath of anti-Yanqui Castros who define others by their previous commitments. Before waking up to find itself aligned with racial supremacists in wars against African Ho Chi Minhs, the United States might better develop a more coherent policy toward southern Africa. If seriously and consistently pursued, such a policy might then at least offer some hope of minimizing or shortening conflict and of restoring sanity to a situation that contains an enormous potential for destruction.

To do less, to continue to rely on moral clichés and irrelevant gestures, is to run the risk of seeing the poison of racism and violence in Southern Africa increasingly feed back into the troubled race relations of the United States. Are American leadership and society so detached from their own revolutionary origins and so unaware and unable to understand the needs and aspirations of black people at home and abroad that they cannot respond? Within this question lies the full meaning and urgency of southern Africa as it confronts the United States. Central to any positive response must be a recognition that this country has already intervened—on the white side.

# NOTES

1. *The New York Times*, July 1, 1965.
2. See Colin Legum and John Drysdale, eds., *Africa: Contemporary Record. Annual Survey and Documents. 1968–1969* (London: Africa Research Ltd., 1969), p. 302.
3. *The New York Times*, October 31, 1965.
4. The word *"tsotsi"* refers to the young criminal elements in the urban centers, rather professional juvenile delinquents.
5. The Genocide Convention of 1948 includes within the definition of genocide "acts committed with intent to destroy, in whole or in part, a national, ethnical, racial or religious group as such." This may result from "causing serious bodily or mental harm to members of the groups." (Article II, b.) To the extent that the application of apartheid in South Africa damages mental health and limits the development of human potentials, it may be said to constitute a form of psychic genocide.
6. *The New York Times*, October 31, 1965.
7. For a discussion of these problems see the author's "The Exile Condition and Revolutionary Effectiveness: Southern African Liberation Movements" in Richard Dale and Christian Potholm, eds., *Southern Africa in Perspective* (New York: Free Press, forthcoming).
8. See Pierre Pascal Rossi, *Pour une guerre oubliée* (Paris: Julliard, 1969).
9. See Donald Barnett, "Report from Hanoi II," *Ramparts*, vol. 7, no. 11 (April 1969), pp. 49–54: and *Angola. Seventh Year* (London: UNITA Central Committee, 1968).
10. The Revolutionary Government of Angola in Exile (GRAE), the People's Movement for the Liberation of Angola (MPLA), and the Union for the Total Independence of Angola (UNITA).
11. See Eduardo Mondlane, *The Struggle for Mozambique* (Penguin: Baltimore, 1969).
12. United Nations, *Statistical Yearbook 1967*, 19th ed. (New York: 1968), p. 115.
13. Address by Hon. G. Mennen Williams, Williams College, Williamstown, Mass., March 18, 1965.
14. *Ibid.*

15. See *The Department of State Bulletin,* vol. 60, no. 1558 (May 5, 1969), pp. 394–395.

16. *Ibid.,* vol. 61, no. 1580 (October 6, 1969), pp. 297–302.

17. Statement by Hon. G. Mennen Williams to the Subcommittee on Africa of the House Foreign Affairs Committee, March 1, 1966.

18. Address by Hon. G. Mennen Williams, Fourth Annual Leadership Institute, Collegiate Council for the United Nations, Chicago, April 18, 1964.

19. Statement by Deputy Assistant Secretary of Defense Frank K. Sloan in letter dated April 2, 1963, Ref. I 3719/63.

20. Theodore Sorensen, *Kennedy* (New York: Harper and Row, 1965), p. 538.

21. *The New York Times,* July 4, 1964.

22. *Statistical Abstract of the United States, 1964,* 85th ed. (Washington, D.C.: U.S. Government Printing Office, 1964), p. 258.

23. *Statistical Abstract of the United States, 1969,* 90th ed. (Washington, D.C.: U.S. Government Printing Office, 1969), pp. 252 and 790.

24. *Washington Post,* May 11, 1965.

25. *Mozambican Revolution* (New York), vol. 1, no. 3 (1964).

26. *Diário de Noticias* (Lisbon), November 22, 1969.

27. *Abstract, op. cit., 1969,* p. 811.

28. *South African Digest* (Pretoria), January 14, 1966.

29. *The South African Financial Gazette* (Johannesburg), June 17, 1966.

30. *Ibid.,* January 15, 1965.

31. See report on survey by AP correspondent Kenneth L. Whiting, *Mercury News* (San Jose, Calif.), February 9, 1969.

32. See Sheila T. Van de Horst, "The Effects of Industrialization on Race Relations in South Africa," in Guy Hunter, ed., *Industrialization and Race Relations, A Symposium* (London: Oxford University Press, 1965), pp. 97–140 and 254–270.

33. *The New York Times,* January 1, 1966.

34. *Abstract, op. cit., 1969.* In 1968 American imports from and exports to metropolitan Portugal totalled $88 million and $86 million respectively. *Ibid.,* p. 809.

35. *The San Francisco Chronicle,* September 10, 1969.

36. *The New York Times,* September 22, 1969.

37. See *Washington Notes on Africa,* vol. 1, no. 11 (1969).

38. *Statistical Abstract of the United States, 1965,* 86th ed. (Washington, D.C.: U.S. Government Printing Office, 1965), p. 947: and *The Star* (Johannesburg, weekly edition), March 5, 1966.

39. *The New York Times,* March 5, 1969.

40. Even if one assumed that the bases were truly indispensable, there is reason to question whether the United States should pay rent in the specific form of political support for Portuguese colonial policy. In the somewhat cynical words of a British journalist: "It is doubtful in any case if Portugal could actually expel the U.S. Air Force and Navy from Santa Maria against their will, any more than Castro has managed to force evacuation of Guantánamo." Russell Warren Howe, "Showdown in Southern Africa," *The New Leader,* February 28, 1966.

41. For its part, Portugal has felt free to purchase Cuban sugar in defiance of American susceptibilities. *The New York Times,* November 4, 1964.

42. *Digest, op. cit.,* January 21, 1966.

43. *South African Summary* (New York), October 6, 1965.

44. The reactor was dedicated in August 1965 in the presence of Dr. Alvin Weinburg, director of the Oak Ridge laboratory. *The New York Times,* August 6, 1965 and *South African Summary,* August 11, 1965.

45. During 1969 the United States-South Africa Leader Exchange Program, Inc., brought to the United States twelve South African couples in the fields of education, journalism, religion, business, and government service. None were African. See the program's *Eleventh Annual Report, 1968–69* (Philadelphia), pp. 5–6.

46. *Sunday Times* (Johannesburg), January 2, 1966.

47. *The Department of State Bulletin,* vol. 60, no. 1554 (April 7, 1969), pp. 301–303.

48. *Ibid.,* vol. 61, no. 1586 (November 17, 1969), p. 424.

# Conclusion: The Racial Dimension of United States Intervention in Africa and Asia

*George W. Shepherd, Jr.*

Charges of racism have increasingly entered foreign policy debates in the United States. The Vietnam crisis has brought these considerations to center stage, accelerated by the growing attention given to the militant advocates of nonwhite power. Events such as the My Lai Massacre and the Bobby Seale trial are only surface episodes in what is becoming a soul-searching process for thoughtful Americans disturbed by the abuses of power in executive authority that have led to colossal diplomatic blunders and tragic domestic conflict.

To cut through this confusion it is necessary to find an interpretation of foreign policy which enables us to perceive the racial issue in terms of behavior as well as attitude. Moreover, it must be based upon a view of foreign policy which links domestic politics and external events. Racism, as discrimination against a hereditary group, may be embedded not only in the attitudes of decision makers but also in the historic institutions and policies of a nation. It can even be found enshrined in conceptions of the "national interest."

Clearly racial conflicts in the social system, as reflected in foreign policy and race relations, form an important dimension of the interaction of political systems. The international system is itself structured by the character of race relations in its component parts, as Max Gluckman pointed out in 1955. Here we are interested in two questions: (1) How does the system of racial discrimination in America affect foreign policy? and (2) is the world stratification pattern a substantial external factor shaping the character of American policy?

Sociologists Shibutani and Kwan in *Ethnic Stratification: A Comparative Approach* present a tremendous amount of empirical evidence to demonstrate that we live in a racially stratified society, both in the United States and in the world. Since the Industrial Revolution, the white races of Europe have pushed outward. In the process they have created white dominance states such as the United States, Canada, Australia, and South Africa, where they have suppressed nonwhite racial groups into subordinate roles.

Looking at the international system as a whole, a wider racial stratification system can be perceived. The developed nations are white while, with few exceptions, the underdeveloped are nonwhite. Conquest, immigration control, and economic growth have been the principal instruments in the creation of both white dominance states and international racial stratification. Motives have been diverse, ranging from economic exploitation, imperial glorification, and escape from tyranny, to a civilizing mission. But the result has been that a number of wealthy, technologically advanced white dominance states economically exploited and colonized most of the world in the eighteenth and nineteenth centuries. They now face a revolt of the subjected that is having wide reverberations within the sanctuary of their own domestic racial stratification systems.

Although colonialism has diminished, technological change has created a stratified world in which the white Western man owns and consumes an increasing proportion of the wealth and the colored majority of mankind has fallen increasingly behind.

The essence of white dominance is a "discriminatory reward" system that favors Anglos and restricts nonwhite mobility and achievement within the system. Apartheid in South Africa is the fullest development of white dominance, while the United States, United Kingdom, Australia, and Rhodesia practice variations of a racial stratification system favoring whites.

United States history of the subjection of nonwhite minorities, from the enslavement of the black man to the subjection of the Indian, is one that historians no longer glorify in terms of the advance of civilization. The white dominance system of the United States was particularly molded by the exclusion of the Oriental. As R. D. McKenzie indicates in his study of *Oriental Exclusion*, admission into the West Coast was halted even before the far western states entered the Union. Immigration and conquest policies often have the same result, that is, the subordination of minorities. The Mexican-American war resulted in large land acquisition and the subordination of a significant Spanish-speaking, nonwhite group in the westward drive of the Anglos.

Much emphasis has been given to the breakdown of stratification in the United States. However, this has been achieved for only a few. The vast majority of American blacks, Chicanos, and Asians have not been integrated into the American society, and if the findings of the Kerner Commission are correct, Ralph Linton's prediction of the eventual disappearance of the American Negro is quite wrong. Ethnic and racial groups are rediscovering and consolidating their identity, from Polish-Americans to black Americans. American society has entered a period of tremendous awakening of these groups whose identity quest now spills over into foreign policy. In our relations with the nonwhite nations, this racial stratification has important symbolic, as well as direct, meaning. Our racial minorities are beginning to respond to what they perceive as the basic racial injustice of the United States interventionary policies in Asia and Africa. Many American nonwhites view the oppression of the black man in South Africa as an extension of their own problems. Their concern is reflected in a Spring 1969 Gallup Poll of American opinion on apartheid in South Africa which showed the percentage of black Americans who were dissatisfied with present United States policy on apartheid to be twice that of white Americans. Similarly increased nonwhite opposition to supporting the war in Vietnam has swelled the ranks of the peace movement and has given it a domestic racial aspect.

### The Pacific

The racial dimension of United States intervention in the Pacific stems from the colonial system we helped to erect there during the nineteenth century. This system was predicated on a "manifest destiny" idea that is both racial and cultural. President McKinley's vision that God willed the United States to seize the Philippines was inspired by the social Darwinist notion of Alfred Mahan that colored races in the Pacific had not evolved political systems equal to those in the white Western world and therefore needed our guidance. President McKinley may not himself have been a racist, but he promoted a political system of colonialism that was in large part motivated by the racial presumption of the superior governing skills of the Western white man.

In the second half of the twentieth century the "manifest destiny" idea still structures both liberal and conservative views of American responsibility in the Pacific. The paternalism of colonialism and the civilizing mission has been replaced by the idea of monolithic communism and the "domino theory." A number of inside memoirs like that of Townsend Hoopes demonstrate that the intellectual advisors to a series of presidents have viewed the weaker cultures and economies of Asia as incapable of standing up to communist, internal, and external pressures. From Korea to Vietnam, American military and economic power has been deployed on behalf of these weaker societies. Men like W. W. Rostow and Gen. Maxwell Taylor developed a complex mythology of defense necessities based upon the assumption of communist ambitions of world hegemony from the defense of Formosa to the Bay of Tonkin.

United States intervention in Vietnam arose precisely because United States leaders could not accept the self-determination of the Geneva Accords. Thus the old Pacific colonial model has been transformed into a security model which is still a racially stratified system. White Americans are defining the nature of freedom and security in the Pacific and are finding Asians who will endorse and enforce these views. Continued United States intervention in the Chinese civil war has been based on this principle. This racial arrogance fuels the strategic myth that American society would be threatened by communist governments in Vietnam and Taiwan. Distrust of Asian capacity for self-rule has become a fear of Asian inability to resist communism, and the old "yellow peril" has become a "red peril" threatening the white democratic world's frontiers. References to "the irrationality" of the Chinese made by high officials in the ABM debates reflect the underlying racial attitudes that reinforce the racial structures of intervention.

Vietnam is not just a mistaken judgment or even a pardonable ethnocentrism but is derived from deep structural white dominance. It is characteristic of racially dominant groups that they are the last to see the sources of their conduct. Many liberals have lent themselves to a racial system without being aware of it. American liberals as well as conservatives have difficulty in accepting this dimension of our behavior, as the American mind has a self-righteousness about its purity of motives.

American nonwhite minorities, however, have begun to probe and to initiate wide criticism. This process was slowed among Asian Americans partly because Japanese Americans were intimidated by the 1945 concentration camp experiences. In addition, like the Chinese, they have been far more successful economically and professionally than Negroes and Mexican Americans. Younger Asian Americans, though, are becoming active leaders in opposition to United States white dominance in the Pacific. Increased protest has been stimulated by the racial exploitation of poor blacks, who have carried a disproportionate share of the fighting in Vietnam as well as the loss of social services at home. Black Americans have begun to challenge the white college deferment system as well as the draft itself, and they have found wide support in sections of the white community. However, the killing of two black students at Jackson State College by police in 1970 illustrates the brutal reprisal action certain sections of the white community have taken against students who protest the inequities of the draft.

### Southern Africa

The United States structural racial link to the white supremacy regimes of Southern Africa may be the racial issue that will generate enough protest to force a recognition of this dimension of our policy.

In principle, the United States is not sympathetic to south-

ern African white supremacy but it is systematically linked to
the white Atlantic security-economic system that preserves a
colonial relationship with Southern Africa. Portugal clings to
its colonies in Africa by force of arms, and British ties in
Southern Africa are racial as well as economic.

Rhodesia has been able to flaunt official United Nations
sanctions only because she is sustained by South Africa and
Portugal, which in turn are a part of what might be called
the white Atlantic subsystem. American mineral firms such as
Union Carbide have pressed for the continuation of United
States' recognition of Rhodesia. American businesses continue
a rapid pace of investment in South Africa and Portuguese
territories and comply with the racial separation laws which
many American businessmen endorse. American technicians
are helping South Africa build a "peaceful" atomic capacity.
In addition, South Africa enjoys an official sugar quota from
the United States government. American General Motors
trucks are quickly converted into military vehicles although
there is a ban on the export of military materials to South
Africa. A military tracking station is maintained by the United
States in South Africa, while black American diplomats are
not welcomed in this land of apartheid. South African vessels
participate in NATO naval maneuvers, and strategists such as
General S. L. A. Marshall claim that South Africa's control of
the strategic Cape route is essential to Western defense.

American relationship with Portugal's paternalism is even
closer. Direct and indirect military aid is given to Portugal
under NATO for the use of the antiquated Azores bases. American oil firms are developing large concessions in Angola, and
the tax revenues from these firms are helping to pay the cost
of Portugal's counterinsurgency campaigns in Mozambique,
Guinea-Bissau, and Angola.

The structural ties with continuing colonial racist regimes are major, thus the United States is already involved in the racial colonial wars raging in southern Africa.

The cold war syndrome that argues the necessity of defending southern African areas from liberation by African communists equipped with Chinese weapons fits readily into a kith-and-kin sympathy with beleaguered whites who are fighting for "civilization." Thus the same strategic rationale used in the Pacific is readily employed to justify policy aimed at maintaining, if not justifying, a racial system in southern Africa. The intent of United States policy is not be perpetuate white supremacy, but the total effect of revenues from American businesses and military assistance is to sustain it.

If the effect of American intervention in Asia and Africa is to reinforce a racial structure conceived under nineteenth century social Darwinism and if this policy suppresses nationalist movements in the name of anticommunism, then the policy has a racial dimension. The road to Vietnam was paved with the proverbial good intentions, but the unjust racial stratification of this world can be rectified only if we are prepared to change systems as well as attitudes. The marginal importance given by the Nixon administration to the United Nations 1971 International Year against Racism and Racial Discrimination illustrates the priorities problem in United States policy.

The racial issue in foreign policy is scarcely recognized at all by policy makers, and where it is, cold war and military security concerns override it. Yet this is a factor that cannot be ignored because of the growing importance in domestic politics. And the problems of United States policy abroad are insoluble without our recognition of the racial dimension of United States dominance. Until United States power abroad is transformed into leadership for liberation, our priorities will be inverted and our major energies will be dissipated in unjustified racial conflicts at home and abroad. The twentieth century is apt to be historically remembered for the emergence of the nonwhite majority of mankind from colonialism. Those countries whose power has been exerted on behalf of liberation will be honored by generations to come.

Courageous policies against racial discrimination are primarily moral in origin, but they have a very practical basis of mutual interest. The respect of mankind is more important than all the sophisticated defense systems and economic aid programs. Our race relations stand at the very center of our self-respect and the world's attitude toward America. We desperately need to improve our capacity to understand and control the impact of race relations on national unity and foreign policy.

# Index

ABM debates, 224
Abraham, Peter, 154
Adamic, Louis, 62
Aden, England and, 183
Africa, American Negro interest in, 167–176, 183; anti-Americanism in, 55, 178; "civilizing mission" in, 151; Communist China and, 156, 195; counter-racism in, 150–163; liberation movements, 194–195, 215; Portugal and, 25, 51–52, 153, 154, 182, 186, 190–193, 198–200, 203, 226; racism in, 150–153, 158; Soviet Union and, 195; tribal communalism in, 152; United States and, 53, 161–185; and Vietnam war, 199. See also South Africa and specific countries
African Methodist Episcopal Church, 168
African National Congress, 194
African nationalism, 4, 150, 151, 154, 192
African Presence, The, 86–87
African Revolution, 195
African Studies Association, 88–89, 205
Agency of International Development, 52
America (see United States)
American Association for the Recognition of the Irish Republic, 63

American Commission on Irish Independence, 63
American Council for Judaism, 67
American Indians, 84
American Negro Leadership Conference on Africa, 51–52, 175, 205
American Negroes, 11–12; citizenship rights, 80, 82, 86; concern with Africa, 167–176, 183; education, 83, 85, 86; housing conditions, 83, 85; income of, 83–84; in key national posts, 89–90; mortality rate, 84; national image of, 89; nonassimilation of, 89; post-Reconstruction period and, 85; repatriation schemes, 84, 91; in Revolutionary War, 42–43; and Vietnam war, 56–57, 73–77, 225; visits to Africa, 168–169, 173
American Revolution, Irish colonists and, 62; Negro soldiers in, 42–43
American Society for African Culture, 87
American Sociological Society, 88–89
American Zionist Emergency Council, 67
Amerindians, 28
Anderson, George, 199–200
Angola, 51, 179, 182, 190, 194; coffee production, 194–195, 203, 209; colonialism, 23; guerrilla action in, 194; nationalist move-